"A wonderful book! Teh writes from the heart about families and life, and nails the humour in all of it."
Kevin Cowherd, Columnist, Baltimore Sun

"Teh demonstrates control over her narrative, and seamlessly employs humour alongside a fascinating exploration of the many interstices of Malaysian life: how we see ourselves and the subtleties of our emotional landscapes. She has a keen eye for Malaysian lunacies and hypocrisies."
Eric Forbes

"... a collection of amusing observations of Malaysian life and its complexities. Through vignettes, [Teh] explores every aspect of Malaysian life, including pregnancies, family, motherhood, festivities, pets and looking for parking spaces. With self-deprecating humour, Teh's candid tales bring to life the warm humour of Malaysian life with all its ups and downs."
The Star

"... [an] amusing, freewheeling journey through the mundane and the everyday. [Teh's] anecdotal musings range from her attempts to live in harmony with the crows of Klang to her love affair with melodramatic Spanish telenovellas on TV. [She] writes with wit and an observant eye trained on all facets of Malaysian life. ... It's just the thing to perk you up on a rainy day."
New Sunday Times

Life's Like That

Scenes from Malaysian Life
LYDIA TEH

Pelanduk
Publications

Published by
Pelanduk Publications (M) Sdn Bhd
12 Jalan SS13/3E, Subang Jaya Industrial Estate
47500 Subang Jaya, Selangor, Malaysia
website: *www.pelanduk.com*
e-mail: *rusaone@tm.net.my*

1st printing 2004
2nd printing 2007

Perpustakaan Negara Malaysia   Cataloguing-in-Publication Data

Teh, Lydia
    Life's like that: scenes from Malaysian life / Lydia Teh.
    ISBN 967-978-886-5
    1. Malaysia—Anecdotes.2. Malaysians—Anecdotes.3. Cultural
    sociology—Anecdotes.4. Social life—Anecdotes.I. Title.
    959.5

Printed and bound in Malaysia

for Kay Yeow, my love and appreciation, always,
and for Tze Wei, Yen Nee, Tze Ren and Su Yen,
more than words can say.

contents

In the family way

Blessed are the children

Leisurely pursuits

acknowledgements

THANK YOU ...

Kay Yeow, for keeping quiet when I get carried away.

Tze Wei, Yen Nee, Tze Ren and Su Yen, for being grist for the mill.

Family and friends, for their support, moral or otherwise. (If you see yourself in these pages, that's "otherwise".)

Chong Sheau Ching, for giving me a head start.

Lim Cheng Hoe and Chan Lai Hun at *The Star* for their cordial cooperation.

The New Straits Times, *The Star* and *www.e-homemakers.net*, for granting me permission to use the articles for this book.

Eric C. Forbes, for his boundless enthusiasm and encouragement, and for breathing life into this book.

And God, for seeing this through.

preface

ALL RIGHT, I'll cut to the quick with
this so you can dive straight in. This book is a compilation
of pieces written over a 10-year period, beginning
sporadically in 1995 and gathering momentum in 2003.
Most of the pieces first saw the light of day in *The Star*,
The New Straits Times and my Bamboo Tales column in
www.e-homemakers.net, and I am most grateful to the editors
of these publications not only for their kind permission to
reproduce and reprint them here, but also for having given
me the space to air my views and parade my prose.

Why do I write what I write? It's a response to things
that happen in my life, a way of coping and letting off
steam. It's a chronicle of everyday events that may seem
humdrum but when put in writing, they are worth more
than the sum of words.

These stories were written from the perspective of an
ordinary, homegrown Malaysian, the quintessential
woman-next-door, so to speak. If you're passionate about
the Malaysian way of life, then this is the book for you.
Though the experiences, observations and perceptions are
mine, they could just as easily be yours for the simple
reason that we share a common heritage as Malaysians.
However, if you're a foreigner, you may wonder and laugh
at the quirks, idiosyncrasies and foibles of Malaysians.

But it is my hope that this book transcends race and culture to reach out to those beyond our shores to share the joy of being Malaysian. After all, the world is a borderless global village and we are citizens of one earth.

If these stories make you smile in remembrance, nod your head in agreement, see familiar things with new eyes or gain fresh insights, then you and I would have made a connection. Whether you're a true-blue Malaysian or a foreigner, I hope you enjoy reading this light-hearted book as much as I have enjoyed putting it together.

VOCATIONAL CALLING

tale of a journey

ONCE UPON A TIME, I worked as a secretary. I was contented with my job. My boss was understanding, the office was just 15 minutes' drive away from home, the pay was satisfactory, and the work was manageable. A pretty good deal, I must say.

Then, I got married. I had my first baby two years later, followed by number two 18 months down the road. I continued to work while my mum babysat my children. I rushed home every evening at five to see my children.

A strange affliction began to beset me. I call it "tibia ironitis" or in layman's language, "iron legs" which I dragged to the office every work day. I dreaded waking up in the morning. On rainy days, I called up the office to take a couple of hours off so I could sleep in a little more. Every little sniffle sent me scuttling to the doctor in the hope that I could procure an MC and stay home with a valid excuse. In short, my heart was not at my workplace. It was at home where the kids were.

I mulled over the idea of resigning but my husband didn't think we could afford to live on one income. "You'll have to get some part-time work," he said.

It was at that time that somebody sold me a set of children's encyclopaedia and roped me in as a direct selling representative. A few months later, I resigned from my office job. My boss surprised me by offering me part-time employment.

A full-time boss with a part-time secretary? I wasn't sure how it would work out. Since he was willing to give it a go, so was I.

Based on my current salary, we worked out an hourly wage. My official working hours were eight in the morning to one in the afternoon. (Company hours were between 7.30a.m. and 5.00p.m.) If I had to work extra hours, I would be paid overtime but I didn't get the regular benefits due to a permanent employee. I could live with that.

My boss was inconvenienced with this arrangement. When he came in, I wasn't there yet. In the afternoons, he had to get other secretaries to help out. My part-time stint lasted nine months. It was a challenge to fit nine hours' work into five hours. Most days I got home by two in the afternoon, sometimes later. I enjoyed my shorter working hours but the pace was too hectic. Eventually I bade goodbye to my eight-year job.

With my office career out of the way, I concentrated on selling children's encyclopaedia and still had time for my preschoolers. I even managed to earn a four-figure commission on some months. After a while I fizzled out. Selling wasn't my cup of tea. My tendency to take rejection personally dampened my morale.

At about this time I found out that the Managing Director under whom I had worked for eight years had set up his own consultancy firm. He needed an extra pair of hands to help with the office administration, so I joined him as a part-timer. I worked once or twice a week depending on the workload.

Meanwhile I had decided to take up a writing correspondence course. The memory of my English teacher reading aloud my essays in class probably had something to do with this latent ambition. Signing up for the course was a decision three years in the making. I finally took the plunge in 1995. My intention to complete it in one year was waylaid by my third pregnancy with its accompanying quirks.

After baby number three's arrival, I quit my part-time office job and became a full-time homemaker. I didn't have the energy or time to delve into anything else. During the duration of the correspondence course, I wrote sporadically and some articles broke into print.

I eventually got my writing diploma five years after I started the course. I began to write more, not that I needed that piece of paper to prod me on. I just didn't take it seriously until my husband insinuated that it was time to earn back the four-figure amount I spent on the course. I even wrote a book. It took a year for *Congratulations! You Have Won!* to see the light of day. It would have been sooner if not for my fourth pregnancy bumping things up a bit.

That put a brake on my freelance writing career, if you can call it that. My definition of freelance writer is "a writer who writes when she's free." On the year that my youngest child was born, I wrote a grand total of three articles.

My baby will be three this year. I'm cranking out the pieces regularly again. No more hiatus from writing sine I'm not going to have a fifth baby. God willing, I'll keep writing till the cows come home.

not as easy as ABC

IF YOU THINK being a kindergarten teacher is as easy as A-B-C, you are wrong. Recently I helped a friend at her kindergarten for a week so that she could go for a well-deserved holiday. To my dismay I discovered that teaching kindergarten isn't kid's play. Though it's a job that doesn't require high academic qualifications, it's a prerequisite to have patience that can stretch to the moon and back.

That singular week of teaching 20 five-year-olds induced the equivalent of one year's stress of caring for my two preschoolers.

Two kids are enough to make me gnash my teeth in frustration. Twenty of them surrounding me three hours a day, five times a week, left me hyperventilating and eagerly awaiting the sweet sound of the bell heralding the end of class.

The children's various antics and choruses of "Teacher, how to do?" transformed me into spiderwoman busily climbing invisible walls. They also brought out the ogre in me, which terrified me but not them.

The black sheep who frazzled my nerves were only a handful but combined with a dozen other inattentive kids, it was tantamount to having my senses assailed by scores of TVs and radios, all tuned to different channels.

Topping the list of nerve-rackers was Yee Meng. Throughout the entire session he would be doing anything except his schoolwork. He wore a perpetual blank look on his face which would infuriate even the most patient of saints. His workbooks were full of uncompleted work, inchoate writing and unintelligible scribbling.

Then there was Beng Teck, the chatterbox of the class. I was continually interrupted with "Teacher, she took my sharpener", "Teacher, Ravi pinched me", or "Teacher, I got Power Rangers at home". Besides the Power Rangers, he has an amazing array of other toys which found their way into his school bag.

Once he brought a plasticene-shooting pistol and the sticky blob landed on the wall above the softboard. As it was out of reach, I left the blob to adorn the wall until gravity brought it down. There was alternative artillery-tank and guns, dinosaurs galore and miniature figurines, all of which I confiscated till the end of the class.

Adrian, who sat near Beng Teck, had angelic looks with manners to the contrary. He was constantly running around the class liked a harried hare but when it came to doing work, his speed slowed to a tortoise's. And his exercise book! If there was ever an award for the scruffiest book, he would win it hands down. His book was pockmarked by little holes caused by vigorous erasing and columns of cellophane tape lined the middle of the book to tape the pages into place.

Hani has mild manners and beautiful handwriting that was painstakingly penned. But she infuriated me with her constant "Teacher, nice or not?" after every row of writing. As there are 10 rows in a page, in the span of half an hour, I had to hear that refrain 10 times!

Another interesting character was Mark who was always eating from his lunchbox during lessons. When recess came, he could still eat the snacks provided by the kindergarten. His metabolic rate must be very high as his frame was pencil-thin.

His neighbour, Yan Mei, would do anything for him. If his pencil dropped to the floor, she picked it up. When he called for an eraser, she immediately produced one for him. When his assignment was completed, she would hand it in to me. I wondered what she saw in him. Maybe it's the food which he so willingly shared with her. Well, they say the way to a man's heart is through his stomach. So it is with the fairer sex, it would seem.

To keep the children out of mischief, I doled out pages after pages of handwritten work. I only realised I had overdone it when the children complained, "Teacher, my hand pain!"

When that week which seemed like an eternity came to a close, I was glad to bid farewell to the stressful job. But as I hugged the children goodbye, I couldn't help the tears pricking my eyes. So, even though I emphatically say to my friend "never again will I teach in a kindergarten", my resolve may just melt away with the passage of time.

The short stint has imbued me with a new respect for kindergarten teachers. Hats off to this wonderful breed of educators who can handle 20 boisterous children daily and still stay sane.

a long shot at fame

WHEN you are not a cookbook writer or in the same league as J.K. Rowling, a book-signing session can turn out to be a lonely affair, believe me.

The beer advertisement showing a leather-clad hunk signing copies of his book while a long queue snaked up the stairs is nothing but hype, trust me, unless you're famous like Hillary Rodham Clinton or a "ghostwriter" who's built up a following like Russell Lee.

It's not that I want to pour cold water on aspiring and new authors but take it from me; I've been there and done that. I can only turn green when reading reports of hundreds of people lining the streets to get the former first lady's signature on her new book, *Living History*. Or of crowds thronging the mysterious masked author who's given Malaysians and Singaporeans 11 editions of *True Singapore Ghost Stories*.

When I attended the book-signing session to mark the publication of my book, *Congratulations! You have Won!*, two years ago, the venue was as empty as a classroom on a public holiday. I shouldn't have been surprised at the turn of events, though. After all, the national pastime of Malaysians is eating, not reading. If there was an open house at some VIP's residence with plenty of free food thrown in, you'd definitely find a crowd there. Not at any book-signing event, unless you're Jeffrey Archer or Stephen King.

A meet-the-author session, book-signing, book launch or whatever name it is called, can turn out to be an ego-buster for an obscure author, unless he is a fantastic publicist or has a book of the same calibre as those in the Harry Potter series. Otherwise, don't build castles in the air. They will come crashing down faster than the motorcyclist hurtling down from atop a skyscraper in the Ministry of Transport's "drive safe" advertisement.

My publisher had arranged for three book-signing-cum-talk sessions. The first was held in Penang as I happened to be there on holiday. A table and a chair were placed near the entrance of the bookshop. As shoppers strolled in, a handful came by to have a look. Most couldn't be bothered to even take a glance. It was as if I was invisible. I talked to those who stopped by and persuaded them to buy my book. It brought back memories of my direct-selling days as a sales rep pushing children's books and encyclopaedias. Fortunately my family was there to lend moral support.

The second session was held in Subang Jaya, Selangor. The store had arranged a table and a few rows of chairs for the audience. They even rigged up a PA system. Problem was, there was no audience. The proprietor of the nearby stall selling CD cleaners was encouraging: "You have to go and say something. After that, people will come." That turned out to be an untruth but I don't hold that against him. This time round, my own family wasn't at the scene, but my brother-in-law, who lives nearby, came with his family.

The final talk was in Kuala Lumpur where the mother of all bookshops was located. Great place, nice ambience, lousy audience. Sure, there were a few people who were seated but some were busy browsing through the books whilst others sat with their arms defensively across their chests, as if to say: "No matter what you say, I'm not going to buy your book."

I know what you're thinking: "There's no pleasing some people. No audience, she complains. Give her an audience, she gripes." That's because you don't know how many copies I signed on that day—but I'm not telling.

However, I was very encouraged by someone who had turned up just to see me. He had bought my book earlier and came to get my signature. (It turned out that Dinesh had just written a book on the same subject as mine. What a coincidence!)

Sad to say, those dismal book-signing sessions were a reflection of how well my books were going to sell. I have to accept the fact that my book is not good enough to make it on any bestseller list. Perhaps the content is not comprehensive enough. Perhaps the writing style is too simple. Perhaps the subject matter is too narrow.

Which leads me to the question of what books *do* Malaysians buy? Scan through the bookstores' bestseller lists and you'll find that about half of the top titles in the non-fiction section are cookbooks (no surprise there, really; after all, our national pastime *is* eating). In the fiction category, the likes of John Grisham, Tom Clancy and J.K. Rowling top the list.

If I want my royalty cheque to sport a bigger figure, I should either write a cookbook or a tale to rival that of Harry Potter's adventures. The first option would entail hounding my mother and mother-in-law for family recipes unless I fancy compiling a "cooking for idiots" guide using my own simple ideas. Then I'd have to badger my photographer brother to snap the requisite mouth-watering pictures. If I take the second route, I have to pester my 12- and 13-year-olds for ideas. I've been asking them: "What do you want to read?" Each time, the reply is "Dunno" or a shrug of the shoulders. That's the trouble with adolescents: when you ask them for input, they've got nothing to say; when you don't, they've got plenty to shout about.

Maybe I should take a leaf out of Rowling's books and scout around for a caf, that'll let me hog a table for hours with just one drink while I write my bestseller. Apparently, she wishes that she could become invisible so that she could go to her favourite caf, and write incognito. I'm one up on her there. I can plonk myself down anywhere and nobody would bat an eyelid. Perhaps there's hope yet for this struggling writer.

LIFE'S LIKE THAT

door-to-door encounters

I WAS WALKING towards the coffeeshop the other day when someone stepped right in front of me. It was a young man in rolled-up shirtsleeves and tie, one shoulder sloping down under the weight of a bulging black bag.

He shoved something into my face. *"Scuse me, ma'am. Letmeintroduceyoutothisthingamajighere. It'sveryuseful, apenwhichdoublesupasatorchlight."*

Exhale.

I wasn't sure if I had caught the drift of his bullet-train sales pitch but one look at the object he was holding told me all I needed to know.

With a terse "No, thank you" I hastily walked away. I dared not show even a flicker of interest for fear that he would pounce on me, tearing up all objections as to why I do not need a pen-cum-torchlight.

Don't get me wrong. I have nothing against these sales people. They make an honest living. In fact I admire them for their tenacity but if you have ended up with the things I have bought from these guys, you would be more wary too.

The first item I ever acquired from these shoulder-sloping salesmen was "The Ultimate Trivia Quiz Game Book". I had no idea what induced me to buy that thick tome of Q&A. I thought the book might come in handy when preparing for Family Day games. It would show the boss that he didn't know the answers to everything.

Take this question, "What void did Captain Hanson Gregory Crockett create in 1847?"

Answer: "The hole in doughnuts." Huh! I doubt even the employees of Dunkin' Donuts' would know the answer to that.

How about this one? "What was the device for city dwellers patented in 1972 by Henry Doherty of Wayne, New Jersey?"

Answer: "The poop-scoop for dog's excrement." It has been five years since I bought that book and I've only used it once—in the course of writing this piece.

Not long after, another salesman came knocking on the office door to peddle the Handyman's 15-piece tool set. It was a little black box containing one fat, yellow and black screwdriver complete with two rows of sockets and socket adaptors.

I was so bowled over by it that I bought two boxes of the tool set, prompted by the words "Perfect as a gift idea" printed on one side of the box.

One set was for my other half who is a DIY enthusiast and the other set was for a friend's birthday. How many times has hubby used it over the years? About once a year, he said.

On another occasion, I bought a cardboard castle which houses a dozen mini books of children's tales such as *Sleeping Beauty* and *Cinderella*.

Alas, when I inspected the goods later, I found that there were two *Puss in Boots* and no *Snow White!* The fair maiden was as good as gone with the salesman.

All purchases from door-to-door salesmen were bought when they called at the office or approached me at eating outlets. Never when they came knocking at my house. Two encounters several years ago had made me wary of them.

In the first incident, a sweet young thing with long straight hair framing a fresh-looking face came knocking on my door. At the gate she said she wasn't selling anything and that she was only conducting a survey. Then she asked for a drink of water, which I felt would be churlish to refuse.

I let her into the house and gave her a glass of water. Did she drink it? Oh no. She proceeded to drop a tablet into the glass. No, it wasn't effervescent vitamin C. She merely wanted to demonstrate how dirty my water was.

Aahh, her intentions suddenly became as clear as filtered water. She was selling water filters, even though she had earlier asserted she wasn't selling anything. The liar!

She made herself so at home that she played with my baby who was lying on his bassinet in the living room. Feeling uncomfortable that a perfect stranger was playing *"anggooo-gooo, anggaaa-gaaa"* with my baby, I led her out to the porch. Still, she wouldn't leave.

I proceeded to sweep the porch, hoping she would get the message that I was busy. Despite the swirling dust from long sweeping strokes of the broom, she continued to extol the virtues of her water filter.

I stood my ground because I just could not afford to blow a few hundred ringgit on a water filter. If it had cost a two-digit price, I would have bought it to get rid of her. Finally, she got the message and left without making a sale.

The other encounter was with a pimply young man who came to my house without carrying any goods to ply. His proposition was too good to be true. Test his company's cookware and I get to keep it just for telling them how it performed. There was no catch whatsoever, according to him. So he told me to wait for the van carrying the cookware to call at my house.

A couple of hours later, the young man turned up again. I told him the van hasn't arrived. Wait for it, he said. Then he came up with another interesting offer.

He held up five cards which he called "lucky draw tickets". One of them was a lucky ticket giving away a free electrical appliance such as a table fan. The other tickets offered discounts on various other appliances. But I had to fill in a form with my personal particulars to qualify for the draw.

I promptly did it and picked a card. I waited with bated breath as he looked at the card I had chosen.

With a sly smile, he said, "Congratulations. You have won a 50 per cent discount for this thermal pot."

The card listed the normal price as RM399, which meant that the discounted price was still RM199. I was sure I could get it cheaper elsewhere. I refused to buy it.

"But you have to. You have already drawn the ticket. It's company regulations. If you don't, I'll get into trouble."

Coolly, I asked for the form I had filled out earlier. He handed it back to me. I ripped it up into pieces.

He was so stunned that when I asked him to leave, he complied without any objection. Needless to say, the phantom van did not turn up.

These days, when some stranger who looks suspiciously like a salesperson ring my doorbell, I just ignore him and let him think nobody's home.

signing for service

IF YOU HAVE DINED in a packed Chinese restaurant with bad acoustics, I am sure you'll agree that the experience is like eating in a school canteen during recess. With the incessant chatter of diners and the clattering of crockery bouncing off walls like ping-pong balls, you probably walked out of the restaurant with a buzz in your ears and an ache in your head.

Add to that the problem of communicating with harried waiters zipping around tables like they were on roller skates, and you get a double headache.

It helps if you know some sign language with which to communicate with restaurant helpers. It saves time and breath as you could sign to a waiter at the other corner of the room rather than wait for him to stop by your table.

Let's start at the beginning. When you enter a popular restaurant at peak hours, you may have to wait for a table to be vacated. When you see someone beckoning for the bill, you quickly move over to "chup" or book the table before someone else does. You stand back politely as the diners get up to leave. The chairs are vacated but the seats are still warm. You stand around waiting for the seats to cool and the table to be cleared. Five minutes later the table still looks like a battle zone strewn with chicken bones, skeletal remains of a fish, fibrous vegetable stems, and tattered tissues amidst a disarray of dishes.

Eye contact is the name of the game here. You lock eyes with a waiter. Without uttering a word, you "tell" him to clear the table by doing a circular motion with your index finger pointing downwards at the table.

The waiter comes with a folded sheet of tablecloth tucked under his arm. He gathers up the dirty tablecloth with everything in it as if he is wrapping up a gigantic *wonton* and deftly spreads out the clean sheet of tablecloth.

At last, the coveted seat is taken and you could rest your arms on the clean table. The waiter goes off to the kitchen with his bundle of dirty dishes. You wait for the captain, the man or woman with notepad and pen in hand, to appear at your side.

You catch sight of a captain a few tables away. You scribble something in the air, the sign that you want to have your order taken. He hurries over with poised pen and pad to take your order.

The order is taken and duly dispatched to the kitchen. Meanwhile, the waiter lays the table with teacups, bowls, chopsticks, the obligatory little plates of red chillies and bottle of soya sauce. Ten minutes pass. Then another 15. There is still no sign of food. You watch incredulously as food is being served at the next table where the diners had arrived after you. And here you are, still facing a food-less table.

You catch the eye of the captain. There is no need to add an angry, complaining voice to the din of the den. Holding on to the gaze of the captain, just point to your watch and spread your hands up with a jerk of your head indicating "Where's my food!?" One look at your empty table and the captain would get the message that you are about to explode like an overblown balloon. He dashes off to the kitchen to hound the cooks.

Finally, just when your stomach is beginning to sound like a gurgling stream, the bowls of rice and steaming dishes arrive. You tuck into your food. It tastes great. In five minutes flat your rice bowl is empty. You want a second helping of rice. You beckon to a waiter and cup your hand upwards as if you are holding a bowl and the waiter will get the cue.

If your tea needs to be cooled with ice-cubes, which now come in the shape of cylinders and so should be called ice-tubes, you curl up your fingers into an "O" shape. If you are worried that the waiter might misunderstand you, then mouthing the word 'ice' will guarantee that your message gets across. Of course, you would have to mouth "peng", "shuit" or "ice" depending on whether your waiter understands Hokkien, Cantonese or English. You have to be circumspect here, otherwise you risk offending the Myanmar or Filipino waiter who might think you were telling him off with the four-letter s*** word when you say "shuit".

When you finish your meal and want to clean up, requesting for tissue is as easy as rubbing your hands together or pretending to wipe your mouth. Amidst the popping of plastic tissue wrappers, you ask for the bill by scribbling in the air again. It's the same sign as asking for your order to be taken but the different context of a littered table render a different meaning to the sign. Usually this chore takes very little downtime unless the cashier has been sleeping on the job. In the time that it takes you to fish out your wallet, the bill would have magically appeared at your side.

So the next time you walk into a crowded restaurant, be ready to let your hands to the talking and you will enjoy your meal better. After all, you should conserve your energy to the task at hand, which is to eat with gusto and not to be irked unnecessarily by overworked waiters.

wet market mania

ONE DAY I went to the morning market and was greeted with chaos. At the lane outside the market proper, the dried goods seller was frantically loading baskets of onions, potatoes, anchovies and other foodstuff into his lorry.

Nearby, the fishball hawker was chucking trays of fishball, fishcake, tofu and everything on his makeshift stall into his van. Other regular traders were not there.

I was puzzled at first—until I saw several uniformed men making their way towards the lane. These unlicensed traders were trying to escape the arms of the law which could slap a hefty fine on them and wipe off a week's earnings with the stroke of a pen.

Welcome to the local magic show where municipal council officers play David Copperfield. They do not need any special equipment to perform disappearing acts. Before you can say, "abracadabra", the traders have vanished with their goods.

After the officers have left, slowly, the errant pedlars would reappear. The shoe seller and clothes trader would spill out of the vans parked across the road.

The noodle hawker would drag her formica table from behind a closed door in the shop where she had taken refuge. The side lane and five-foot way would soon be resuming their usual hustle and bustle.

Wherever there are markets, roadside stalls would invariably spring up, offering a wide array of foodstuff and merchandise to market-goers. In my residential area, these stalls revolve around three markets housed in two rows of shophouses located back-to-back. Competition is keen amongst the three markets, especially between the two vegetable sellers located along the same row of shophouse.

This is especially apparent whenever there is a vegetable glut and the two vendors have to fight like cats and dogs for business. One vendor would hang large cardboard tags advertising super low prices. Sometimes they would shout at the top of their voices to attract customers to their stalls.

"Cabbage! Cabbage! One for 50 sen!"

However, not all the market vendors are competitors. Some are bound by family ties. There are two husband-and-wife teams in these three markets.

The pork seller in market A is the husband of the pork seller in market B. The chicken seller in market B is the husband of the chicken seller in market C. Such an arrangement can work out to the customers' advantage.

Once I wanted to buy some whole chicken legs from the chicken seller in market C but she had run out of them. Not to worry though. She whipped out her plastic-wrapped handphone and rang her husband.

"Eh, you got five whole chicken legs? Got-*ah*? Okay, send them over here." Mission accomplished. I got the chicken legs without having to visit the other market.

During peak hours, the pace in the market can be frenetic. With a dozen customers all clamouring for their purchases at the same time, a sense of humour helps vendors to keep their sanity intact. A case in point is the pork seller in market C who has a ready smile and wicked wit. Someone recently commented on the lack of choice cuts at her stall.

"If you want better choice, you should go to my husband's stall. There's more variety there. Women like to go there to see my husband. He doesn't wear a shirt. If I don't wear a shirt, a lot of men will come here to buy pork from me," she said with a smile. "Just joking-*ah* ...."

On hearing her remark, the crowd of papaya-faced customers who were weary of waiting broke into wide grins. It was true that her husband, a small but well-built man does not wear a shirt at his stall in market A. He only wears white tennis shorts with a white cloth draped across his stomach for an apron.

The fishmonger in market A is another specimen with a funnybone. A couple had asked for half a kati of big prawns. With scrunched-up newspaper in one hand, the other hand scooping up prawns with a plastic bowl, he said in English, "No-*lah*. Half kati is too little, the prawns will swim away very fast. Better take one kati." The couple paid for one kati without protesting.

This particular fishmonger knows his trade well. Not only is he an expert in cutting and cleaning fish, he has more than a basic knowledge of cooking which he uses to persuade customers to buy his fish.

When I come across an unfamiliar fish, I would ask him how to cook it. He would launch into an express cooking lesson ala Chef Wan.

"This fish should be fried. Pound some garlic and ginger. Fry them, add some soya sauce. Then pour the gravy over the fish. Best!" he said while giving the thumbs-up. I swallowed my saliva and bought the fish.

If ever Mr. Fishmonger decides to change his profession, he should seriously consider following Chef Wan's footsteps. In fact, he does resemble the bubbly chef somewhat.

Most market-goers are women but sometimes there's the odd male or two. They belong to either of two categories, experts or novices. "What are those black spots on the cauliflower?"— that's a novice. The experts would have deftly picked up the vegetables without conferring with the vendor.

Unlike women, men don't dilly-dally. They may arrive at the stall later but while the women who were there first were still scrutinising and poking around, the men would have paid for their goods and zipped off.

If you want to catch up on the latest gossip, the market is the place to visit. It could be about the poor old lady who died when a snatch thief accosted her and pushed her to the ground. Or it could be a housewife regaling her friends with tales of her recent trip to China and how she was ripped off by unscrupulous traders.

The next time you go to the market, keep your eyes and ears open and you would be treated to an array of rich and colourful sights and sounds (and who can ignore the smells?)

waxing lyrical
over 'raisins'

MY THIRD AUNT was the official ear-digger of my family when I was young. She lived next door to us. Every now and then, she would march in and demand to dig the ears of whoever was around.

My siblings and I did not mind giving in to her demands. If anything, we eagerly awaited our ear-digging sessions.

Third Aunt plonked herself down on the floor. Sitting cross-legged and wielding the spoon-shaped metal ear-digger, she was like a dentist attending to her patients. The difference is the patients relished the occasion, not abhorred it.

I lay down on her lap with my head turned to one side. She pulled my ear with one hand while the other hand probed with the ear-digger.

As she scraped out the ear wax, she placed them on my open palm. It was such a pleasurable experience that I nodded off only to be jolted awake by a sharp pain when she scraped too hard or poked too deep. After she had dug out the "gold" from one ear, she tapped me on the shoulder, the signal for me to offer the other ear.

When I became old enough, I began to dig my own ears. To avoid any nasty surprises, I sat far away from anyone else. The ear-digger was inserted into one ear. With head tilted towards the direction of the ear being dug and eyes half-closed, I scraped out the wax gingerly. Aahh ... what a divine feeling, like finally managing to reach a spot which itched and scratching it.

Now I have graduated to the role of official ear-digger in my own family. Initially I performed the task on my older children only as I feared that my young son would imitate me by poking pencils into his ear.

We locked ourselves in the bedroom where the small boy could not see us. The bedroom lights were dim, so I had to use a torchlight to get a clearer view of the ear canal. As one hand was used to pull the ear and the other to hold the ear-digger, I had to alternate between shining the torchlight and digging, a clumsy operation altogether.

The solution to this predicament presented itself one day. My husband had bought a mini headlamp for our eldest son's school trip to the caves. As I couldn't find the usual hand-held torchlight, my eldest son lent me his mini headlamp. What a useful gadget it proved to be! I strapped the headlamp onto my head and adjusted it so that the light could shine directly into his ears.

My husband burst out laughing when he saw me. I didn't care that I looked ridiculous. What was important was that I had a clear vision of the ear canal. I could see wax clinging to the walls like crumbs of *tausa pneah* (round biscuits with crumbly green bean filling). With the anticipation of a miner digging for coals, I plunged into my mission with great delight.

Lately I've taken to digging the ears of my five-year-old son. But not before admonishing him that "only mummy can do this, you cannot put anything into your ear." He nodded and put his head down on my lap meekly. He was very ticklish and squirmed this way and that.

After he settled down, I started to clean his ear. At first only little fragments were excavated. Then I hit pay dirt—it was something hard and huge. I couldn't see it though. Slowly and gingerly, I tried to scrape it out. Nothing doing. It seemed to be firmly lodged inside the canal. I tried again, a little harder.

"Pain, mummy," my son murmured.

"Okay, mummy will be gentle. A little bit more. It's moving, yes, it's coming out. Don't move Jin-Jin."

I could see the wax clearly. It was a black lump, still stuck inside the ear. I grimaced as I tried to coax it out without hurting him.

"All right, it's coming out. Slowly now, it's going to be out, okay. A bit more, just a bit more. There it is!"

Was I relieved! I felt like a doctor coaxing a baby out of the birth canal during labour. I showed the black lump to Jin-Jin.

"It looks like a cockroach egg, doesn't it?" I asked.

"No, it looks like a raisin," he said.

Now I'll have to think twice before popping another raisin into my mouth.

tales from the mobile zone

WHAT do managers, *cendol*-sellers, businessmen, fishmongers, remisiers, college students and housewives have in common? The mobile phone, of course.

Gone were the days when handphone toters used to get envious looks from the have-nots. In today's high-tech, high-speed world, a handphone is a necessity to keep in touch, to get ahead or to get that juicy gossip across.

"So what if you got handphone, I also got what," any Muthu, Ali or Ah Chong can snigger.

Surely we have, at one time or another, come across a cartoon strip that showed a handphone ringing and everybody whipping out their handphones from their handbag, briefcase, pocket, haversack or whatever.

These days handphones come with personalised ringing tones making it easier to identify one's own call. From a catchy excerpt from the William Tell Overtures, more popularly known as the "Lone Ranger" theme song, to simple beeps, from loud rings that can be heard a few floors away to mere vibrations, it is easier to individualise handphones to eliminate the dozen "hellos" chorusing in answer to one ringing tone.

Most men carry handphones in their bare hands. Some like to hook them onto their belt. For this type of hands-free carrying, the phone must be ensconced in a PVC case with a clip. Invariably, one gets the impression that the phone-on-the-belt guys are contractors, entrepreneurs or salesmen.

Mobile phones sheathed in plastic casing need strong fingers for dialling. If you have used one before, then you will know what I'm talking about. When you thought you've pressed all 10 digits and are ready to hit the "send" button, the LCD showed that only four digits have registered because your finger did not exert enough pressure. How much pressure then? Think of typing on a manual typewriter and you'll get the idea.

The fishmonger's method—wrapping the phone with a transparent plastic bag and securing it with a rubber band—is the best option if one is more concerned with protecting the handphone from wear and tear than following the latest trends. It looks ugly—somewhat like a wrapped-up fish package—but scores high on functionality, plus the phone doesn't end up smelling like old socks.

Mobile-phone users can be loosely categorised into three groups. The first is the Phua Chu Kang type.

"Hello, Frankie-*aah* ... How's my business? Of course, very good-*lah*. Best in Singapore and JB what, and some even say Batam. How much I quote for Mr. Lee's jacuzzi? Eh, you think I so stupid to tell you-*ah*?" And the conversation can be heard miles away in JB.

The second category is the Casanova. The speaker is so discreet and utters his words in the hush-hush tone that you think he's whispering sweet nothings to his lover. Even if you were to stand beside him, you would not be able to make out a single word that he says.

Finally, there's the "diamond in the mouth" type. Right from the time he presses the green button to "talk" until he presses the red button to end the conversation, he would go "aha, mmmm, uh, ya, huh," all the way through. Not even a "hello" or a "bye" lest the diamond comes rolling out of his mouth.

For safety reasons, the authorities have made it an offence to use a handphone while driving. The driver must either pull over to the roadside or use a hands-free kit. Hence you see motorists zooming around with wires dangling from their ears, seemingly yakking away to themselves. A sight stranger than Martians? Not quite, but almost.

It is even more peculiar when you see these people with earphone wires hanging around their neck when they alight from their vehicles. It brings to mind doctors with stethoscopes. Maybe it's a fashion statement of some sort but it can be pretty dangerous. What if there were muggers around? These no-gooders could easily use the wires as a convenient weapon to strangle their victims. It's better to be safe than sorry, so stash those wires away from sight even if it may be a tad inconvenient.

It is ironic that while the handphone is to enable people to keep in touch, many institutions are banning its use in their premises. Of course, they have their own reasons such as safety, consideration for others, blah, blah, blah, but it's downright inconvenient to switch them off. Just look at the number of places they're banned from—banks, lecture halls, libraries, petrol stations, hospitals, cinemas and so on.

Most people disregard the "No handphone" signs put up at the entrance except at hospitals where it could mean life or death when handphone signals could interfere with life-saving equipment. Other than that, it's really no surprise when in the midst of a lecture, while queuing up at the bank or during that exciting car-chase scene at the movies, a "beep-beep" sounds loud and clear, followed by an even louder "Hello!"

aim for the impossible

NADIA COMANECI, the world's first
perfect gymnastic scorer, wrote her autobiography when
she was 20. While browsing through it the other day, this
paragraph grabbed my attention. "It is unbelievable what
can be achieved if you only try. Aim for the impossible."

This can-do attitude need not be confined to lofty
ambitions but is applicable in everyday life too.

The following day, I went for a swim. For years I have
kept to the shallow end of the swimming pool. My
excuses for staying away from the deep end were lack of
stamina and not knowing how to tread water.

With Nadia's advice still reverberating in my mind, I
decided to take the plunge, literally. From the shallow
end, I traversed the edge of the pool until I reached
somewhere in the middle which was more than 1.8 metres
deep. I took a deep breath and kicked off. After a few
strokes, I noticed that the water ahead was a darker shade
of blue.

Then I saw it. Underneath, the gradually sloping
floor suddenly dipped a few feet down. The cold from the
deeper depths of water engulfed me. My heart thumped
furiously. I steeled my nerves and swam cautiously
towards the pool end. Each time, I dipped my head
underwater, I tried not to look down at the floor. I made it

to the pool end without stopping. Yipee! From then on, the deep end was a phobia no more.

A few weeks ago, I triumphed over a mundane but monumental task (at least it was to me): opening the "king of the fruits". My father had given me some durians and not wanting to wait till hubby return from work for the "opening ceremony", I decided to make my debut as durian opener.

Armed with a knife and some rags to hold the thorns at bay, I carefully cut along two lines leading to the apex at the stalk. Exerting an extra ounce of strength, I managed to pull the wedge apart. Unfortunately, that was the bad sheep of the family. Brownish stains spotted the edge of the fruits and before I could say "Yummy", a big, fat worm reared its head at me. I threw that wedge away, and opened the rest of the durian. My reward: thick, creamy fruits that were worth the wriggly encounter. Talk about enjoying the fruits of your labour!

Another occasion when I had "aimed for the impossible" was during a trip to Fraser's Hill. My husband, some friends and I were going up there for a church seminar. Hubby had sprained his ankle a few days earlier while imitating a Foo Kok Keong stunt at the badminton court. As our friends' car was not available, our ancient Volvo took to the road.

Since I am liable to succumb to motion sickness during long winding journeys, I decided to put to test the notion that drivers are spared from nausea. I had never driven along the treacherous, winding road that leads up to Fraser's Hill. Quelling my fear of driving down a ravine on the way up, I drove all the way from the New Klang

Valley Expressway to the summit and whaddayaknow?
Nausea never had a chance and we arrived safely.

Yesterday I witnessed an impossibility turning into a
possibility. This friend of mine has just entered the
insurance profession after years of coaxing from her
Million-Dollar-Round-Table husband. She never
envisioned herself selling insurance. But she took up the
challenge though she was still unsure of her selling ability.

I was present during her first sales presentation. After
listening to her sales pitch and interjecting with a few
questions, the potential client simply said, "Okay-*lah*." I
was amazed. That was it! The sale was in the bag in a mere
quarter of an hour.

What was it that Nadia wrote about achieving the
unbelievable if you would only try?

mother's hospital stay

MY MOTHER was warded at the hospital recently. She had been complaining of dizziness and nausea for two weeks. As her visits to the general hospital had not resulted in any improvement, I took her to a private hospital for a checkup. The doctor admitted her immediately and ordered a battery of tests. The results were not good. Mum is a diabetic with hypertension and high cholesterol. Her blood glucose, blood pressure and cholesterol level were sky high and, according to the doctor, these were affecting her brain. She remained in the hospital for a week until her condition stabilised.

The anxiety of waiting for test results, worrying that mum might be diagnosed with a terminal illness, hanging around the hospital for hours waiting to see the busy doctor and dealing with the incessant phone calls from family and friends was a stressful experience for me. Mum, on the other hand, was quite upbeat and seemed to be more concerned about how she would pass the long hours at the hospital with nothing to do.

Mum didn't want to be placed in a twin room. She wanted to be in a four-bedder as it was cheaper and she would have more company. She struck up a conversation with an old woman who had earlier consulted the same doctor as her. It turned out that she was to be admitted too. Later we bumped into the old woman's son at the cafeteria. I asked about his mother's rooming arrangement.

"My mum wants to stay in a room with many people. She's scared to be alone," he said.

I explained that my mother wanted company too and was hoping to be warded together with her. He obliged by giving his mother's name. At the admission counter, the clerk checked at the computer and found that the particular ward was already full.

Mum need not have worried though. As it turned out, the ward she was admitted to had a roomful of elderly Chinese patients. At 60, she was the youngest there. When I visited her the next day, she was in good spirits and had made friends with her roommates. Her neighbour on the left, Ngor Cheh, who was warded for asthma, was just like my mum—talkative. The lady on the right was quieter. The 82-year-old woman across the room was asleep most of the time, tended to by a young Indonesian maid.

Ngor Cheh was a good companion to mum. Though she didn't mince her words and kept reprimanding mum for her cavalier attitude towards food, she was likable. Both mum and Ngor Cheh didn't look sick and sometimes they talked so loudly and animatedly that I wondered if they didn't bother the other patients.

Mum called Ngor Cheh a "hot girl" as she would powder her face, pencil her eyebrows and apply lipstick everyday. Ngor Cheh often joined in the conversations mum had with her many visitors. When the dietitian went to see mum, she listened in as well and could tell me what had transpired between them.

The dietitian had left a diet guideline which listed over 80 foodstuff to avoid. I read out the list to mum. When I came to mangoes and bananas, mum commented, "I don't eat a lot of bananas. Only one at a time."

Ngor Cheh, who had been listening quietly, bristled and exclaimed "One banana! You should only take one bite, not one whole banana. Really, it's quite pitiful. There're so many things you have to abstain from. But that's not to say you can't eat them at all. When your glucose level is lower, you can eat them, but just one mouthful each."

"One mouthful. I'd rather not eat it then," Mum muttered petulantly.

Ngor Cheh shook her head like one would when confronted with a spoilt child.

The other inmates were not as vocal as Ngor Cheh. The patient on mum's right suffered from swollen feet due tc her diabetes. She was quiet and smiled politely when she saw me. The frail old lady whom everybody called Por Por slept through most of the day but some nights she kept others awake with her groaning. The maid who had slept upright on her reclining chair until mum taught her how to recline the chair, blissfully slept through the night.

I felt sorry for both the maid and Por Por—the maid for being cooped up in the hospital 24/7, and the old lady for the intense pain she suffered due to *kut chee*. I'm not sure what's the English term for this ailment but one thing was certain, it's an extremely painful condition judging from Por Por's intermittent "*Aiya*, it's so painful." Though she was immobile, her brain was far from senile. A visiting friend had heard her calling out a long list of names, presumably that of her family members. Mum also told of how the maid had made Por Por a cup of diluted coffee on doctor's instructions but the old woman had detected the inferior taste and scolded the maid.

One day as I was about to leave the ward, I heard Por Por calling out "Ah Cheh!" which means Big Sister in Cantonese. I approached her and asked if she was calling me.

"Call you also, can. Anybody also can," she groaned. "Here, here," she said as she pulled down her blanket. She pointed to her sarong which was knotted tightly at the top.

"The sarong's too tight," I told the maid. "She's feeling uncomfortable." I was about to loosen the sarong when the maid stopped me.

"No, don't do that!" she said. "She will take it off and expose herself. I feel so embarrassed."

I explained to Por Por why she must keep her sarong on, but she didn't appear to understand. I left her grumbling at the maid. I heard that Por-Por would be discharged in a few days after a two-month stay at the hospital. I hope she would do better at home.

Ngor Cheh was discharged a day before Mum. With her gone, the ward was very quiet. Mum is home now. Though it had been a stressful week, our lives had been enriched by the concern shown by family and friends and the interesting people we've met at the hospital.

pseudo-truths

PSEUDO-TRUTHS. Yep, we've heard them expounded so frequently that they often masquerade as universal truths along the line of "The sun rises in the east and sets in the west."

What are you yapping about, you ask? Statements like this, "it always rains after I washed my car."

Okay, so the car hasn't been washed in weeks and the relentless hot weather has coated it with a layer of dust, thick enough for graffiti to be drawn on it. So you decide to pull out the hose and give the car a thorough shampooing. You're still admiring your handiwork and the gleaming paintwork when the heavens open up and send down a torrent of rain.

"Spot on!" you exclaim if you're an irregular car washer like me. Of course, if you wash your car everyday, this statement can only be true if it's uttered during the rainy season.

"The other queue always moves faster." This seems to apply more to hypermarket check-out counters than anywhere else.

Say you arrive at the cashiers to find that there's a queue at every counter. Naturally you join the shortest line. If the queue has the same number of waiting customers, you survey their trolleys to see which line has less items to be checked out. Steering clear of those with laden trolleys, you take your place behind the lady with half a basket of purchases.

As the cashier rings up the last two items, the lady with the basket discovers that a bag of oranges had not been weighed in and priced. So back to the fresh produce section she goes to get it weighed while everybody in line fidget sullenly. By the time she gets back, the other line with the laden trolleys has checked out into infinity.

By the way, there's a solution to this—go shopping in twos. Get your shopping partner to stand in one line while you wait at another. Just wheel over the trolley to whoever reaches the cashier first.

Here's another one which involves waiting. "The traffic light always turns red when it's my turn." Whether you've been queuing for a kilometre or have just arrived at the lights, it always turns red. Of course, this statement only appears to be true because you don't count the times you cruise through the green lights.

A spin-off which is closer to the truth is, once you hit a red light, the next few lights would turn red on you too. Probably this has something to do with the sequencing of the lights. It's particularly annoying to get caught at roundabout traffic lights where your vehicle only moves a few feet before having to stop, three times in a row.

"The phone always rings when you're in the bathroom." There hasn't been a peep from the phone the whole day and you're not expecting anyone to call either. But the moment you step into the bathroom and disrobe, the pesky phone rings and there's nobody to answer it but your two-year-old girl.

"The children always squabble or cry when you're on the phone." This is especially true for work-at-home folks.

And it always happens during work-related calls. It's as if the children have to let everyone know that there's a bunch of active kids running berserk in the home-office.

"A stray tissue always end up in the laundry when you're washing dark clothes." Have you lost count of the number of times you have to shake out the zillions of tissue specks clinging to laundered clothes like flaky dandruff? Now if only you had checked the pockets before loading the washing machine, you wouldn't be in this exasperating situation.

"A humongous zit always sprout up just before an important event." Whether it's your own birthday party, a graduation ceremony or a company's annual dinner where you want to look your absolute best, a pimple the size of a ping-pong ball would materialise on your forehead, nose or cheek.

Finally, here's a personal one for me that concerns my two-year-old daughter. It's not pseudo, it's the real McCoy. Whenever we sit down for a meal, she always wants to go potty. Not once, but twice. The first time is to *shi-shi*. The second for big business.

Of course, the other family members think it's funny because they don't have to dirty their hands.

It's always I who end up doing the dirty work.

when the lights go out

T HE lights go out and the fans stop spinning. Blackout! You check if it's a meter trip. If it isn't, you peer at the neighbour's house to see if they have power. If they don't, then it's time to call Tenaga Nasional's breakdown hotline.

You know you're the first to call if they ask you a host of questions like have you checked your meter, have you checked the neighbour's house, when did it happen, your telephone number and your name. To spare yourself the hassle, wait a few minutes so that other zealous souls can make the report first. You still have to call just to be on the safe side, in case the affected houses are few and nobody in those households reports the blackout.

Our electricity supplier appears to be very efficient these days. Blackouts are rare, at least in my area they are, and when they occur, they only last a couple of hours. Tenaga Nasional had obviously learnt its lesson from August 3, 1996 when a power outage occurred for a whopping 14 hours.

I lived near my mother's house then. Whenever there was a blackout which didn't affect her house, my family and I would make a beeline there. But this particular blackout affected my house, mum's house, the whole residential area, the town, the state and the entire peninsula! When people realised the magnitude of the outage, the situation became mildly chaotic. People rushed out to buy torchlights, batteries, candles, matches, food supplies, gas and petrol.

With no lights, no air-con, no fan, no television, no radio, and no computer in working condition, that ignoble day yawned into the night. The minutes inched by. It made us wonder how our forefathers passed the time without the convenience of electricity. What was there to do at night? Perhaps this is one reason why families of old are so large.

Early to bed,
early to rise,
make a baby,
in the night.

Folks who are used to sleeping with the air-conditioner on are a pitiable lot on blackout nights. Without the cool air, they can't sleep a wink. It reminds me of a church camp held several years back at a denominational centre in Port Dickson. A power failure hit us on the first night. Before the hour was out, a rich family who was visiting with us had checked out of the centre and into a five-star hotel.

I'm glad my children have been raised without the comfort of the air-condition lulling them to sleep. They can sleep through a blackout without batting an eyelid. If it was a warm night, they may toss and turn but they would remain in the Land of Nod, perhaps dreaming that they were traipsing in the Sahara Desert.

As for me, I can do without the air-conditioner but I need the fan like fish needs water.

My siblings and I grew up with 5-speed fans. (Since getting married, I have lowered my standard to 2-speed to accommodate my 0-speed spouse.) In our younger days, we dragged our mattresses into the living room and slept with the front door open to let in the night breeze. When the fans suddenly whirred into life, we whooped loudly with joy if we weren't asleep yet.

We still do. Whoop loudly with joy, clap our hands and make a fanfare of it. So do the neighbours. The resumption of electricity calls for a celebration.

On a scale of 1 to 10, 10 being the pits, daytime blackouts may inconvenience our lives on a scale of 4 perhaps. Sure, electrical appliances may not be working but we can still file, read, write letters the snail way, clean out the cabinets, cook with gas and do a host of other stuff. (For businesses and manufacturers, it's got to be a 10. Ditto for train and LRT commuters—a blackout is a hassle any time of the day.)

It's more tricky at night. We can't see our way around without a torchlight or candles, let alone do whatever it is we do at night. There's the option of visiting some place where there's power such as the shopping centre, the *mamak* stall or mother's place. But if we choose to stay at home, how can we while away the time? Here are some suggestions.

- Have a candlelight dinner. This would be a genuine candlelight affair without the ambience spoilt by a fluorescent light filtering in from somewhere.
- Play shadows on the wall. The kids would love it. Rabbits, dogs and butterflies are easy shapes.

Make some complicated ones and have a guessing session.

- Play board games. During a recent blackout, my children and I spent two hours on Monopoly. Of course, we had to place the candlestands far away from the paper money.
- Conduct a storytelling session on the porch. Light the mosquito coils or incense burners to keep mosquitoes away. Bring out paper or straw fans for keeping cool and for swatting mosquitoes.
- When there's nothing else to do, go to sleep or do whatever it is you do in bed.

say cheese!

I HAVE FEW snapshots from my
childhood. In fact, they can be counted on one hand.

There's one of me as a chubby six-month old baby on
a round rattan chair, another as a scrawny kid perched on
the shoulders of two uncles and one with my mother
standing in front of a lion's statue.

My hubby, lucky him, had chocolate boxes full of
childhood photos taken by his father who was a
photography buff. There were loads of photographs of
him playing with his siblings or out at the park with his
extended family. With his collection, he can run a
marathon down memory lane while I sprint.

In the olden days, a camera was a luxury. During
special occasions such as weddings, family members and
close friends would troop to the photo studio with the
bridal couple for the photo shoot. These were simple
affairs. A few shots of the couple, the bride on her own
and a group photo. And that's about it. What a great
contrast to the 12-hour, 100-pose, 20 costume-change
photo shoots of today.

Photo studios of old have limited props and
backdrops at their disposal. Linoleum covered floors and
curtained walls are as good as they get. A leaf from a palm
tree, artificial flowers, a guitar and the ubiquitous round
rattan chair were some of the props used.

Poses were simple. For bridal or engaged couples, they stood or sat side by side. For ladies' portraits, hands-under-the-chin was the vogue then. Guys added on the charm by donning a cowboy hat. These portraits would be distributed to family and friends. Selected ones were enlarged and mounted in black frames to adorn the living room walls.

Outdoor shots were usually taken during excursions. Girls would be lined up a flight of steps or stood slanting in a straight row. Poring over my mother's yellowing photos, I'm struck by her slim figure. Back then, everybody was slender. At worst, pleasantly plump but never obese. The girls looked svelte in their dresses with gathers at the waist and the guys appeared smart in *"engkee"* drainpipe pants. But I digress.

It's a different picture today. With affluence, every other family can afford to own a camera or two. Modern technology has given us the digital camera with which we can snap as many shots as we want without wasting money on developing spoilt pictures.

We take pictures of every occasion, celebratory or otherwise. Weddings, birthdays and parties are never complete without a cameraman in attendance, sometimes more.

Infants, particularly firstborns, are another favourite subject. Pink-faced from labour, all scrunched up in their swaddling cloth, proud fathers snap reels of films of their bundle of joy. As the infants journey through the first year of their lives, countless pictures are taken to chronicle every momentous step of the way. As the babies grow up, go to kindergarten, school and university, there would be milestone shots of first days, concerts, class parties, graduations and more.

Not packing a camera for trips, especially overseas vacations, is tantamount to leaving out a chapter from our book of life. It is imperative to record memories of where we've been, with whom we've had fun and the unique sights at each location.

Everyday scenes make interesting snapshots too. A child riding a bicycle in the park. A mother feeding a baby. A get-together with friends. A cuddle with a furry rabbit. Such photos will imbue our album with an ordinariness that turns poignant with the passage of time.

Pictures abound of happy and important moments and to a lesser extent, ordinary events. What about sad occasions? Do people take pictures of a seriously ill person or a funeral? Except for professional photographers, few people would do so. The reluctance may stem from "a time and place for everything."

Actually it may be a good idea to snap photos of funerals, especially if the deceased had lived to a ripe old age. It would serve as a historical record of sorts for the family. But I would stop short of shooting the deceased lying in the coffin. I would rather remember him as a living person than a pale lifeless face.

I remember browsing through some old photos of a friend's father's funeral. Grief showed in stooped shoulders and bowed heads. It was a reminder of the frailty of life and the pain of bereavement. Alas, sorrow is an inevitable part of our lives.

Whatever the reason behind the picture, it freezes that singular moment for posterity and accumulates into a treasure trove of memories.

what a load of rubbish!

WE USED TO HOLD the record for the tallest building in the world. That honour now belongs to Taiwan for the Taipei 101 building. But we have another record unscathed: Malaysia has the biggest dustbin in the world: the roadside.

I see the testament to this record every weekday when I send my children to school. The first dustbin is located along what we've nicknamed the monkey road for obvious reasons. This lonely stretch is flanked on both sides by oil palm plantations, thick undergrowth and a couple of housing estates nestled in between. Strewn along the road shoulders are rubbish scattered in all its glorious mess—pink, yellow, orange and blue plastic bags ripped open by foraging monkeys; with leftover food and other household rubbish strewn in disarray after the scavengers are done with them. What an eyesore! Really, this road should be renamed *Jalan Sampah*.

The other dustbin is located along a busy road with *kampung* houses straddling it. Obviously the refuse truck can't enter the narrow lanes of the *kampung* to collect the garbage, so the municipal council provided one of those large trapezoid receptacles for the rubbish collection. But one miserable bin isn't sufficient to serve the needs of an entire village and the shops that lined the road. The spot has become a gooey mountain of multicoloured garbage bags.

The tyre workshop located behind this ugly dumpsite tried hard to clean up the place. I've seen workers clearing up the mess. They put up potted plants to beautify the area and barricade the rubbish from spilling over to their premises but to no avail. Trash kept encroaching upon their grounds like festering gangrene. In the end, it was a case of "if you can't beat them, join them." The last I saw, heaps of old tyres were discarded atop the growing mound.

What is it about Malaysians? That we have first-world facilities but third-world mentality is an oft-spouted line. It's true nonetheless as far as keeping our streets clean are concerned. People don't care where they dump their rubbish as long as it's not at their own premises. What can we do when confronted with such pathetic civic-consciousness?

We could take a leaf out of Bill's book. This friend of mine lives in a semi-detached house and, like most of his neighbours, take pride in maintaining neat lawns and keeping the road outside clean. All except one neighbour. This litterbug dumps his trash out on the road. When Bill confronted him, his reply was, "This is government road. I shall do what I like with it." To spite Bill, he threw out more rubbish on the road. Bill took pictures of the "crime scene" and sent them to the town council with a letter of complaint. The authorities came and slapped the errant neighbour with a summons.

Good for Bill. How many of us would go to such lengths though? We may tell the neighbours in a nice manner but if they don't practise the golden rule of doing unto others what you would have others do unto you, we just end up suffering in silence. Take Bill's sister. She lives in a corner house with a strip of grass patch outside her house. Her neighbour dumped his garden refuse outside her house even though he has his own grass curb. Despite telling him to refrain from his unneighbourly practice, he persists. So she bears with it.

My sister had an inconsiderate neighbour like that too. But it wasn't garden refuse which landed in front of her house but perishable waste such as prawn shells and fish intestines. If only these neighbours are just as generous in sharing real goodies like a nice pot of money plant or a plate of prawn fritters. Wouldn't that make life more pleasant?

I can't keep the front of my house clean either. You see, I live near a school. Plastic bags tied around the neck with straw jutting out, drink packets, junk food wrappers and soft drink cans litter the ground. When I see a wrapper flying out of a school bus, boy, do I get angry. I want to stop the bus, grab the recalcitrant student, force him to retrieve the litter and make him run to the nearest dustbin to dispose it. I want to yell, "What did you learn in Moral studies about not chucking rubbish anywhere you like, huh?"

But I don't. I'm afraid the whole bus of kids may gang up to bully me. I may honk at the culprit if he's at the back of the bus and I could gesture to him. Otherwise, it's a waste of effort as he may think that the horn is directed at another motorist.

Grownups are just as bad, if not worse. We've all seen the spring-cleaning motorist in action, especially at the red lights. Car window whizzed down. Out flew tissue papers, wrappers, parking tickets, plastic bags and what not. I feel like blaring the horn and shouting "Ooei! You think this is your grandfather's road-*ah*?"

But I'm chicken. I'm afraid it could be a road bully lurking inside the car and he'd bash me up. I may press the horn timidly but the targeted recipient might not even get the message.

Where education has failed, regulation might just be the key. But it will only work with enforcement. It's useless to put up signboards prohibiting the dumping of rubbish if the authorities do not nab the culprits and impose a hefty fine on them. We should emulate our neighbour, that "fine city" down south. Thanks to its strict enforcement of litterbug laws, their streets are spick and span. Now, that's a sight for sore eyes.

SPECIAL
SEASONS

wish list

MY KIDS are too young to buy me diamonds or send me on a world cruise for Mother's Day. Not that I'd demand such expensive gifts from them even if they could afford it. What I want is something that money can't buy. This is my wish list for each of my four children.

Eldest son

You're a great help, washing the car and putting up the laundry besides doing your regular chores. But I have one complaint—why must you do them with a face as long as Gandalf's beard? Smile, and I might just reward you with extra pocket money.

And if I choose to tune in to a Chinese channel or play the *Winter Sonata* cassette in the car, would you mind keeping your hands off the radio dial? You can listen to your favourite Mix FM in your own room and cry a river with Justin Timberlake that your mother refused to let you have your way with the car stereo.

One more thing. I know you're all of 13 years old, at that age where you're neither a kid nor an adult. But I would appreciate it if you would talk like an adult. You know, speak clearly instead of mumbling? I don't have the Bionic Woman's ears you know.

Who's the Bionic Woman, you ask? She was the heroine of a 1970s TV show who could lift a car with one hand and hear conversations a mile away, which I can't. So speak up, boy.

Elder daughter

Thank you for helping out with your little sister. I appreciate your initiative in making milk for her and playing with her but I wish you'd change her wet nappy without making a fuss. It's not as if an accidental jab of the pin would make you bleed to death. Besides, practice makes perfect. By the time you become a mummy, you'd have learnt how to pin a baby's nappy so well it wouldn't drop.

I know you're busy preparing for the UPSR but I wish you'd come when I occasionally ask you to help with the cooking. I look forward to the day when you can prepare a meal on your own.

For this Mother's Day, I'll settle for a tuna sandwich for breakfast, thank you.

Younger son

You're so cheerful and outgoing. Some of the things you say can really crack us up.

But please stop asking us about volcanoes. You've asked enough questions about the volcanoes, whether they can destroy houses, cars or people; whether they can erupt on rainy days—if you want to know any more about the volcanoes, please look it up in the encyclopaedia.

And could you please keep your room tidy? Your room looks like a very big laundry basket. Your pyjamas are on the bed, trousers on the floor and towel behind the door. Very soon, you'll have no place to sleep because your clothes are going to take over the room. You know the VCD we watched called *Mars Attacks* where the aliens from Mars attack the people from earth? Well, if you don't keep your room tidy, you're going to get a "Clothes Attack". Your clothes will jump up on their own and tie you up. Don't come screaming for mummy's help when that happens.

Four days after your birthday is Mother's Day. On this special day for me, I don't want you to mention volcanoes. And remember to hang up your clothes properly on the clothes railing without any reminder. You don't want a "Clothes Attack", do you?

Youngest daughter

You bring so much joy and laughter into our lives. Your older siblings love you and like to play with you. Well, most of the time. I hope you don't drive them crazy when you start playing with their stuff later. For now they're quite happy with you.

But when are you going to learn that the potty is the place to poo—not the chair, the play pen or the floor? And could you please let mummy work on the computer without climbing up on my lap?

There's a special day coming up called Mother's Day. Mummy won't be working on the computer on that day so you're welcome to my lap all you want. There's something you can do for mummy on Mother's Day. If you have to poo in your nappy on this day, please do it while mummy is out and daddy is babysitting you.

How about it, kids?

costly tradition

I LOVE the smell of new notes, especially when I get them in little red envelopes called *ang pows*. Every Chinese New Year I looked forward to receiving my annual windfall—until marriage swung me from the receiving to the giving end.

Whilst young people look forward to Chinese New Year in anticipation of *ang pows* galore, married folks greet it with trepidation for the very same reason. Children and singles are the most privileged as they get to pocket the red packets without having to fork out any in return. Their parents are the ones who have to dish out the *ang pows*. Married couples without children incur the heaviest "losses". If these people are stingy, they may suddenly become anti-social during the two weeks of festivity.

Anyone who has prepared *ang pows* before can tell you that it entails more than just having ready cash, though this is THE most important requirement. Bright red *ang pow* envelopes and crisp currency notes are mandatory but these seem to be in perpetual shortage every year. Timing is critical. If you visit the bank too early, you'll be told, "Not in yet." If you go too late, it's "Sorry, no more stock." You have to go at the right time which is approximately two weeks before the festival, give or take a couple of days.

An *ang pow* packet may have the most beautiful designs on its cover but it's the content that is of paramount interest to receivers. It's perfectly logical that richer folks can afford fatter *ang pows* but this doesn't necessarily happen. Wealthy or not, it's easier on the wallet to stick to accepted conventions.

During the 1970s, it was the RM1.10 era. The philosophy behind this is *chut kak*, Hokkien for "jutting out of the corner". It's an august wish bestowed by the giver for the recipient to *chu ren tou di*, a Mandarin expression for doing better than others.

As inflation increased, so did the *ang pow* quantum. Even-numbered denominations, usually RM2, RM4 or RM10 are common. This is in keeping with the Chinese belief that even numbers are auspicious.

Nowadays anything goes. Last year my children received RM3 packets from someone. I can't figure this one out. I know five-ringgit *ang pows* are popular as the RM5 bill makes it a convenient choice. Besides, it's a respectable amount and not as damaging as a red note. But RM3? Maybe it's because three in Cantonese sounds like *sang* which means life.

Several years ago when Bank Negara stopped the circulation of RM1 notes and issued coins instead, it posed a weighty problem for RM2 and RM4 *ang pow* carriers. Innovative banks devised *ang pow* packets that came with a four-slit card to hold the coins. Though that took care of the jingle-jangle and gave the packet a streamlined look, it didn't resolve the weight issue. So Bank Negara's subsequent introduction of RM2 and later RM1 notes was greeted with much relief. That eliminated the need to lug around an additional bag for carrying *ang pows*. Phew!

If ever there's an unwritten law about *ang pow* giving, it's the rule of reciprocity. If someone gives your children an *ang pow*, you should reciprocate to the giver if he has children. Some people use this to great advantage.

I'm reminded of a colleague's Chinese New Year gathering many years back. As my family and I walked into the garden, a co-worker who was also there as a guest, handed out *ang pows* to my two children. He was like the God of Prosperity, sans traditional costume, distributing *ang pows* merrily as though he had a bottomless pocket.

What made me think he was out for a killing wasn't the fact that he had four children. Neither was it the fact that most of us had two children or fewer. It was his strategic position near the front gate to welcome guests as they walked in so as not to miss anybody. The minute we stepped in, we were greeted with "Hello, happy new year. Here's an *ang pow* for you." If he had distributed them while mingling around, I wouldn't have thought anything about it.

Well, I have four children now but perish the thought that I distribute *ang pows* with an ulterior motive. Getting one or two extra packets of *ang pows* compared with smaller families doesn't necessarily mean a "profit", if you know what I mean. I won't do the sums here to prevent this article from reading like a profit and loss statement.

Incidentally, receiving of *ang pows* has its own etiquette too. It's considered rude to open an *ang pow* in front of the giver. This makes good sense as it spares both parties from embarrassment should the amount fall short of expectation.

Some children have been taught to wish, *"Gong xi fa cai, hong bao na lai,"* which means "Wishing you prosperity, hand over the *ang pow!"* *Aiyo,* that sounds so rude and greedy. Whoever invented that greeting ought to be sent to Miss Manners for polishing up his manners. *"Xin nian kuai le,"* or "Happy New Year" is a better salutation.

Whether giving or receiving, keep in mind that it's more blessed to give than to receive. That should cheer up givers though the pocket will be getting lighter. And it should make recipients happy as their wallet will be getting heavier.

swinging into action

WHENEVER the Chinese New Year falls in January, it creates havoc with my time management. Having barely recovered from the year-end holiday season, the new calendar year arrived to usher in the back-to-school rush. Then wham! The catchy tune of *gong xi gong xi* fills the air and crates of mandarin oranges materialise at road side stalls.

It's time to speed things up. I have some serious catching up to do. Better compile a to-do list to stay on top of things.

- Trimmed and fertilised plants three weeks to the day. After a month of neglect, hopefully there's enough time for the fertiliser to induce glorious blooms of bougainvillaea, adenium and Japanese roses, and for healthy green shoots to flourish. Two more rounds to go. Must remember not to overdose on fertilisers or will end up with withered plants.
- Managed to wash all the curtains over a two-week period. Would have gotten it done sooner had it not been the rain messing things up. Now that the weather is bright and sunny, it's time to wash the bed linen and blankets. There's nothing like the fresh smell of detergent to greet the new year.

- Go to the bank to exchange new money and get *ang pow* packets. Have ready smile to coax sullen tellers into parting willingly with crisp bills and red envelopes. Be understanding. There are hordes of demanding customers queuing up for their share, as if the banks are giving out gold ingots for free.
- Send out greeting cards. Keep some spare cards and stamps to reciprocate unexpected cards received late.
- Buy new year goodies like Chinese sausages, mushrooms, mandarin oranges, candies, canned lychees, cordial, etc, for the mandatory exchange of new year goodies amongst family and friends.
- Get the cleaning woman to vacuum away the cobwebs and dust the top of cupboards. It's unlikely that mother-in-law will clamber up these spots to check but it's better to be safe than sorry. Tee-hee! Don't think she'll do that. This is the best time to do spring cleaning so the house will be spick and span to impress visitors.
- Dig up recipe books for ideas on what cookies to make. Might decide to go traditional this year and serve the "tray of togetherness". Candied melons for growth and good health; red melon seeds to symbolise joy, happiness, truth and sincerity; dried lychee for strong family relationships; kumquat for prosperity; coconut candy for togetherness; peanuts for long life; longan for many good sons and lotus seeds for many children. On second thoughts, I might forego the

last two. Already have four children—a large brood by today's standards.

- Buy ingredients for making cookies. Don't be too ambitious. Buy what is needed, period. Remember last year's extra packet of icing sugar for making melting moments? It's still lying around in the larder. Get ready wooden ruler to swat kids' hands if they swipe too many freshly-baked cookies, especially the big boy who has gotten past the age of asking for permission before he guzzles anything he fancies. Wash and dry empty Milo and milk powder tins for storing cookies. (Plan B: if there's not enough time, just buy ready-made cookies.)

- Wash and iron new clothes. Remind the children not to wear all-black or sombre colours to grandparents' house during Chinese New Year. The weather is already sizzling hot, no need to subject ourselves to verbal grilling.

- Make as many trips as needed to hypermarket, morning market and night market to buy whatever stuff yet to be purchased. Must refrain from buying too much as most supermarkets will be open during the festival.

- Get children to make mini lanterns and fish from old *ang pow* packets for decoration. Coax hubby to make origami cranes for hanging on plants. Remind him to take out the string of mini lantern lights from the storeroom and put them up, if they're still working.

- Plan dishes for potluck reunion dinner. If cooking a new dish, experiment before D-day. Remind family members to eat more of own dish so that it's not embarrassingly untouched by the end of dinner (what to do, mother-in-law and sisters-in-law are better cooks). Alternative—cook smaller serving.

- Do marketing early to avoid last-minute rush. Avoid stocking up on perishables.
- Prepare *ang pow* packets. Empty handbag to free space for stashing *ang pow* packets.
- Chinese New Year eve. Rise early, cook early and arrive early at in-laws' to avoid frazzled nerves. Don't forget *ang pows* for the elders.

Have a swinging new year!

ON THE ROAD

parking woes

AFTER CIRCLING through the packed parking lot for the umpteenth time, you finally spot someone about to leave. You flick on your signal light and align your car accordingly, eager to claim the coveted lot. The driver gets into the car and fiddles around with something. Never mind, you tell yourself, what's another two minutes on top of the 15 minutes you have already wasted.

The minutes tick by. Then the driver gets out of the car, locks the door, and walks away with his hands in his pockets. Of all the cheek! He could have waved you off so that you need not have waited in vain and missed other vacated lots. A wave of the hand was all it would take to indicate that he wasn't leaving yet.

Unfortunately, Malaysian drivers can be a devilish lot when they get behind the wheel, right up to the time they park their vehicles. Surely you have come across the following scenarios at one time or another.

You are waiting for an empty parking lot when you see a car reversing out. As you get ready to ease into the vacated spot, another vehicle coming from the opposite direction cruised into the very spot you are eyeing.

Or you might have spotted from afar an empty lot in a congested area. You can't believe your good fortune until you drive closer and see a motorcycle parked majestically in its oversized lot. *Gggrrr* ... Why don't they stick to their own parking bays?

Some drivers, especially delivery truck drivers, are downright inconsiderate. They park their trucks anywhere convenient for them to load or unload their wares with no thought for other road users.

Last week I was caught in a tight spot by one of these trucks. It was parked in the centre of the road, blocking all access as both sides of the road were lined with parked vehicles. There were more than a dozen cartons of bottled drinks that the man and his attendant were unloading for a mini-market.

As I pulled up behind the truck, they cast me a look which seemed to say, "So what can you do about this, huh?" I could just feel the fumes coming out of my nostrils and ears as I reversed out the same way I had come from. I couldn't resist blaring the horn loudly at them. Not that it did any good. With expressionless faces, they carried on their task in slow motion.

Truck drivers aren't the only ones who think they own the road. Some luxury car owners are guilty of this too. Recently I encountered a gleaming black Mercedes jutting out onto the road, blocking one lane of a two-way road. What was worse was that the car was parked in the vicinity of a school and dozens of eating outlets, including some very popular *bah-kut-teh* (herbal pork stew) shops. The place was crawling with school buses and scores of vehicles. But that was of no concern to the Merc driver. All he cared about was parking right at the doorstep of his destination regardless of the inconvenience he may cause to others.

Somehow I had this vision of a balding middle-aged man, sipping his tea and enjoying his *bah-kut-teh* while he revelled in how his Merc was reigning supreme on a busy road. He probably thought that nobody in his right mind would dare risk his own car being damaged by "kissing" his Merc but he has yet to meet the novice driver who might do just that.

Speaking of schools, coffeeshops and other high traffic areas, I pity residents who live near such places and are at the mercy of inconsiderate drivers who park in front of their gates. A friend who lived behind a school once had her entrance blocked for a few hours by a car. When the errant owner returned, there wasn't even one word of apology offered for the inconvenience she had caused.

I have seen house-owners placing those orange and white road dividers in front of their houses to prevent other cars from usurping their right to enter and leave their premises as they please.

Double parking is another common grouse. It is easy to forgive a double parker who has a lightning quick errand to run but those who double park for hours on end really make the blood boil. A friend who lectures in a private college has colleagues who double park and then disappear for hours after lectures, imprisoning the legal parkers.

Then there are drivers who cannot differentiate between horizontal and vertical parking. They park vertically in a side-parking lot, with their vehicles jutting out precariously onto the road. Or they park horizontally in vertical parking lots, taking up two boxes and depriving other motorists of a precious lot.

Besides insufficient parking lots, the other factor that contributes to our parking woes is motorists' aversion to walking. Most drivers like to park right at the doorstep. There may be plenty of vacant lots available on the next road but they would avoid them as if they're strewn all over with thumb-tacks.

Consider this. A gym-goer drives up to the gym, takes the lift up and then only starts to sweat it out on the exercise machines. Ironic, isn't it?

driving through thick smoke and flat tyre

I AM a competent driver. In fact, I dare say my driving skill is at tertiary level. I can weave in and out of traffic to get to my destination soonest possible. I can overtake quickly and safely. I know how to drive bumper-to-bumper without letting another car jump queue. If you were to put me to a PhD-level driving test, I'm confident I can cruise through with flying colours.

But if you test me on the nuts and bolts of the car, I shall fare no better than a kindergartner at algebra. I only know how to pump petrol when fuel runs low. Period. Anything beyond that is Greek to me. What lies beneath the car bonnet has enough mystery to be classified under X-Files. This has landed me in hot water several times.

The most memorable incident happened on my way home from work several years back. My journey home was usually smooth and unimpeded. On that particular day, I got caught in a traffic jam. As I fidgeted in the car, I happened to glance at the temperature indicator: it was just above mid-point. No cause for alarm, I thought, but I was dead wrong. Very quickly, the needle had shot up to HOT. The I spotted a thin wisp of smoke rising from the car bonnet. With pounding heart and sweaty palms, I shot up an SOS call to God.

God really answered my prayers pronto. While debating what to do, I spotted my sister and her husband in their van right behind my car. We pulled over to the roadside. When my brother-in-law lifted the car bonnet, trapped smoke billowed into the air like a giant mushroom. I had never seen anything like it before.

Fortunately there were several car workshops located along that stretch of road. My brother-in-law fetched a mechanic who drove my car back to the workshop. The cause of the malady was easily identified. The water in the radiator had dried up. It was like a desert in there with nary a drop of water.

Not long after this incident, I had trouble starting the car when it was time to knock-off from work. I got the help of the factory maintenance guy who identified the problem as "engine overflow", whatever that meant. The bottom line was this—once the engine has started, it mustn't remain idle, otherwise it will go kaput. He helped me start the car and told me to drive straight to the nearest motor repair shop.

I felt like a Grand Prix driver attempting the most crucial race in my career. From the moment the engine roared to life, I stepped on the accelerator like my life depended on it. I barely paused at junctions, afraid that the engine would sputter dead. It was a wonder that I made it to the mechanic's without any mishap.

Usually I am not very sensitive about my car's behaviour. But one morning while driving to work, I sensed something different about it. One of the tyres seemed to be grating on the road. Then it hit me. I had a punctured tyre!

I was in a quandary. I didn't know how to change the tyre, so what's the use of stopping? Hitching a ride from strangers was out of the question. Neither did I have a handphone with which to summon help. So I decided to continue driving with the flat tyre. After all my office was just a few kilometres away, I reasoned.

A car pulled up beside me, honking to draw my attention. With the driver keeping pace with my car, his companion clapped one hand down over an upturned palm, indicating that I had a flat. I nodded and pointed to somewhere in the horizon, trying to tell him that my destination was drawing near. They smiled and zoomed off.

By the time I reached my office, the punctured tyre looked and smelled like it had been microwaved on high. On hindsight, I should have flagged down those Samaritans in the car. Whether they were good or not would have depended on whether they help me change the flat tyre.

Not long ago, I drove some friends to the theatre to watch a live performance of *Jack and the Beanstalk*. It was raining heavily when we set off, so I switched on the headlights. When we arrived, the rain had stopped and the sun was out. We made a beeline to the theatre. I only realised I had forgotten to switch off the lights when the car refused to start two hours later.

We tried to jumpstart the car but we might as well have tried to raise a corpse. The battery was dead flat. The mechanic had to be fetched to install a new battery.

Recently, hubby commented that my car suspension seemed to be out. He laughed when I replied that I didn't feel anything amiss with it. For me everything is a-okay unless the petrol indicator is flashing a warning. I have driven my car through thick and thin (read thick smoke and thin tyres), what's there to worry about loose suspension? No problem!

make way!

PATIENCE is not a virtue of mine, especially when I am on the road, the operative word here being "road." This is hardly surprising as most Malaysians sprout horns and fangs the moment they get behind the wheel.

Here is a list of drivers who can make the blood pressure shoot up. Keep score of how many drive you round the bend. Check your score at the end of the piece.

1. **The woe-am-I drivers**. A collision has happened. But why-oh-why must the drivers leave their vehicles in the middle of the road to jam up traffic to infinity? I don't get it. With so many people around: victims, onlookers and towtruck operators, surely there are enough hands to push the vehicles to the roadside. The wrecks aren't murder victims that can't be touched in order to allow the police and the forensics team to conduct their investigation. Get them off the road first, then bicker all you want about who's at fault, who's going to pay what and which towtruck gets the business. I have a hunch these hapless people derive some masochistic satisfaction from inconveniencing hundreds of motorists to   · compensate for the hassle they have to go through.

2. **The busybodies**. These are the drivers who slow down to look at accidents. It isn't uncommon for both

sides of the highways to be jammed up even though the accident happened on one side only. Curiosity kills the cat is a maxim that can ring true in such situations. Accidents have happened when cars slow down to get a better look. People can be so inquisitive. How bad is the accident? Are there any casualties? What is the registration number for buying *empat ekor* (four digits)?

3.   **The queue cutters.** I wish for one of those sophisticated cars in James Bond movies, you know, the type with so many gadgets they look like gigantic Swiss army knives. I'm only interested in one function though—press a button and sharp blades would shoot out from the side of the car. Very handy for scratching the queue cutter's vehicle. But I'll let in cars carrying school-uniformed children. They have to get to school on time. This forgiving spirit means I'm also guilty of this misdemeanour. But only if my kids are late for school, which doesn't happen very often. Once or twice a week at the most. On second thoughts, it's a good thing these gadgety cars aren't in the market, or I might end up being the *scratchee* instead of the scratcher.

4.   **The slowcoaches.** When everybody is cruising at 80kph or more, these guys are driving at 50. They could be doing one of three things—yakking on the cellphone without a hands-free kit, talking and gesturing animatedly with the passengers or gazing dreamily into the distance. To avoid from vomiting blood, overtake at the first available opportunity.

5.   **The yellow-box hoggers.** Yellow boxes are there for a reason. They're not drawn by municipal workers struck by a sudden spurt of creativity while painting the roads. For the uninitiated, a yellow box means "do not

stop vehicle in the box." Why? Because they will obstruct traffic. A James Bond car with a forklift mechanism would be useful for lifting the obstructing cars out of the way.

6.   **No-signal drivers.** This breed of drivers is becoming more rampant by the day. They should be sent back to driving school to learn this simple rule: signal left to go left; right, to go right. This applies to overtaking, turning or stopping. If every vehicle's signal lights are used as they should be, there would be less accidents, road congestion and irritation.

7.   **Loud honkers.** Sometimes we make errors in judgment; sometimes we are just plain impatient. A car may be approaching too near at the junction but we take our chance and make a quick crossing, hoping the driver would slow down understandingly. Decelerate they would, unless they fancy a collision, but not before blasting out a horn so loud it makes one jump out of the skin and break out in cold sweat.

8.   **The faint-hearted.** These are the drivers who take the whole day to cross junctions, dare not overtake or hit the brakes when the lights turn yellow. Hello! You stop when the lights turn red, not yellow, which means speed up.

Check your score now.

If you are irked by:

6 to 8 Categories — You're a typical Malaysian driver. Better get a grip on yourself before you end up in the hospital for hypertension. Easy now. Take a deep breath and count to ten ....

3 to 5 Categories — You're neither a devil nor an angel. Keep a check on yourself so that you don't veer off the fiery end.

1 to 2 Categories — You're a saint! We need more people like you on the road. How about setting up a driver's finishing school?

0 Category — You're not real!

UP CLOSE AND PERSONAL

of myopia and paranoia

LAST WEEK I broke my spectacles for the second time in two years so I dashed off to my regular optician. Stanley checked my eyes and announced that the power that is needed for both eyes had decreased yet again.

In my younger days, I would have jiggled with joy. I remember the trouble I went to in order to "cure" my myopia. I was told that looking at green grass in the early morning could remedy shortsightedness. So every morning, I dragged myself out of my cosy bed and cycled to the school nearby.

I stood outside the school fence and stared fiercely at the green, green grass of the field. I couldn't be bothered with passing motorists who must have wondered at the teenage girl perched on her bike, seemingly staring into space.

My eyes looked near and far, far and near and they skimmed along the parameters, every blade of grass stripped bare by my piercing stare. Alas, the dew-clad field was no antidote for my shortsightedness.

Now more than two decades later, my optician is telling me that age has done what the green, green grass had failed to do. Age has an inverse relationship with the degree of myopia, it seems. The higher the age climbs, the lower the myopia dips.

This is no consolation. If anything, it's a bane. Firstly, it costs money to keep changing glasses due to decreasing myopia (or broken lenses).

Secondly, it's the harbinger of a malady that will burn another hole in my pocket—long-sightedness. I complained to Stanley that lately I was finding it difficult to thread needles and read fine print.

He checked my eyes and declared, "You still don't need reading glasses ..." I heaved a sigh of relief, "for another two years."

I exploded. "Two years?! But I'm too young!"

Those fortyish friends of mine whom I've been sniggering at can now laugh and say, "Welcome to the Reading Glasses Club," as they peer at me over the top rim of their spectacles.

"I don't want to wear bifocals!" I muttered as I walked out of the examination room. Stanley reassured me that I don't have to wear those hideous glasses which can age anyone by 20 years.

"Now there are multifocals. They're very nice to look at. No lines, like normal glasses but more expensive," he said.

That's like saying, "You can have your cake and eat it too but the cake's going to cost you an oven."

I have other options, though. I could emulate some friends who own two pairs of glasses. One for shortsightedness, another for long-sightedness. But these are male friends who have their shirt pockets for popping their spectacles in and out of. Perhaps I should revamp my wardrobe and add a breast pocket to all my garments.

Another alternative is to literally wear two pairs of glasses at the same time. Attach each pair of specs to a chain and perch one pair on the nose and let the other pair hang around the neck. Exchanging them would be a breeze. But I'd have to be careful that the specs don't collide with each other during switching. Otherwise, I'd end up with two cracked specs instead of one ugly pair of bifocals.

I would love to wear contact lenses but my eyes are boycotting them now. In the past I had worn them without any problems except for the odd minor mishap or two.

One incident stood out clearly. I was running late for work and just couldn't wear my lenses properly. The left lens felt as if it was donned on the wrong side. This was akin to wearing a shirt back to front, only worse as it causes blurred vision and discomfort. As I didn't want to miss my car pool, I had to dash off, fuzzy eyesight and all.

When I got to the office, I tried to pinch the errant lens out of my left eye. After a few attempts, I realised in horror that there was no lens in my eye! I had been pinching my naked eyeball all along. I must have dropped the lens at home without realising it.

But it was not the eye pinching that spelt the end of contact lenses for me. I think it was the extended wear lens that did it. Extended wear lens is just what their name implies. The wearer could wear it for an extended period of time, not just the twelve hours or so of normal lenses.

Initially, the extended wear lenses were great. They were very comfortable. I even wore them to sleep sometimes, which was a no-no with the normal variety.

After a while, the problems began. My eyes felt as dry as toasted bread. Worse, it hurt to wear them. The transparent discs felt like metal pins in my eyes.

I then decided to take a couple of years' hiatus from contact lenses. After that I tried disposable lenses. It was no better. The same pin-like sensation was there. I consulted an eye specialist who diagnosed that I had some pimple-like protrusions under the eyelid or something, and it's advisable not to wear contact lenses.

After pouring hundreds of dollars down the drain on contact lenses, cleaning solutions and eye specialist fees, I finally bade a reluctant farewell to my tiny transparent friends-turned-foes.

I've resigned myself to wearing spectacles for the rest of my life but hey, there's always laser surgery. Now, that would be another story altogether.

waking up is hard to do

WHEN I was much younger, wild elephants couldn't wake me up from my slumber. My mother used to have a tough time waking me up. Still she found it easier waking me up in the mornings than trying to rouse me from nocturnal sleep.

Those days my father used to buy supper home after dropping off his last cab passenger. My siblings and I looked forward to digging into the oodles of fried noodles but due to the late nights he kept, this meant that sometimes we were asleep by the time he got home. Despite instructions to my mother to rouse me if father brings supper home, inevitably I would wake up some mornings to discover that I had missed out on supper the previous night.

If I accused her of not waking me up, she would tell me that she tried to but that I slept like a pig. For the non-Chinese, this is our equivalent of sleeping like a log. All the hand-pulling, shoulder-tugging and face-slapping couldn't bring me out of dreamland. What was more surprising was that I would have no recollection of the calisthenics that went into rousing me.

When I got married and had children, a 180-degree change took place. If before I slept like a bear in hibernation, motherhood bestowed a catnap's characteristic on my slumber. I became like this young mother whom I read about in a *Reader's Digest* anecdote.

A doctor was preparing to go for his night shift when he accidentally knocked down a metal ashtray. He dived to catch it but both crashed down onto the floor loudly. He held his breath, afraid that he might have woken up his wife and baby. However, nobody stirred.

Then the baby coughed. His wife flew out from their bedroom to the baby's room. After checking on the baby, she came out from the nursery and, seeing her husband lying on the floor for the first time, asked: "What's with you?"

God is wise. When He created women, He stirred in some maternal instincts so that even the soundest of sleepers can wake up to tend to their little ones. Though my babies and I slept in different rooms, the teeniest cry would jolt me from my sleep. Firecracker or thunder I can sleep through, baby's little whimper I can't.

Now that my youngest child is two, the biological alarm clock is somewhat out-of-use. My little girl still wakes me up in the morning with her cry for "Milk! Milk!" but most of the time I have to rely on the radio alarm to wake me up to prepare my preschooler for kindergarten.

The alarm clock is a life-saver. Whoever invented it ought to receive a Nobel Prize. This little gadget has probably saved millions of jobs for sleepyheads who might otherwise have been sacked for tardiness.

It has probably prevented millions of students from being caned for late arrival at school.

For daughters-in-law, it has probably prevented them from being excluded from in-laws' wills by impressing them with their ability to rise early to tend to the family.

However, for the alarm clock to be effective, discipline is a prerequisite on the part of the user. I'm one of those who misuse this useful device which has merged with the radio to become the friendly radio-alarm. Too friendly, in fact. Being roused by a beautiful song can backfire as it could just as easily send one back to dreamland. For people like me who are wont to go back to sleep again, the built-in buzzer which works like the conventional alarm with its jarring "tut-tut-tut" sound, is a sleep-rouser. If only I could refrain from rolling back into bed after switching it off.

I tried to rise and shine early by heeding the Bible's admonition of "Sluggard, go to the ant and observe her ways". Not that I intend to jump out of bed and go ant-hunting in every nook and cranny of the house, mind you. Once in a spurt of zeal, I even pasted the verse on the mirror of my dressing table but its warning that "your poverty will come in like a vagabond" due to "a little sleep, a little slumber and a little folding of the hands to rest" wasn't stern enough to motivate me to become an early bird. The spirit is willing but the flesh is weak.

I read in the papers recently about Hollywood's Celebrity Wake-Up Service which has signed up Pamela Anderson to lend her voice to urge subscribers to "wake up, get down on your hands and knees and bark like a dog." I don't think that line is going to work with me. The vision of our dour-faced Boxer wagging her stump of a tail would spring to mind and that's not a very appealing picture, I assure you.

Pam would probably need to deliver this stinging rebuke in her sternest dulcet voice to get me going. "Every second the sun releases enough energy to supply our planet with power for over a billion years—and you can't get out of bed? What kind of work ethic is that? A bad one, that's what. Now get up, get to work, and fuse with hydrogen, or a least have some coffee." But for US$7.99 (RM31), I think I'll pass.

A better idea would be to get a recorder and tape my toddler's cries of "*Milk! Milk! Milk! Milk!*" Never fails to wake me up unless hubby is up-and-about and I'd just holler "Daddy, make milk for Su Yen!" and sink back into bed.

just loo it!

SOME DO IT every morning. Some do it at night. Some do it only when the urge arises. Some do it at home. Some do it in the office. Some do it when they're about to eat. Some do it right after a meal.

Do what? Big business or depositing money in the bank, or in kiddy-speak, *poo-poo* or *ng-ng*. Euphemisms may abound for this necessary bodily function but when you're sitting on the throne or squatting on the pedestals, you're one of two types: toilet-reader or toilet-thinker.

I'm amazed at how some people can just sit or squat and stare at the walls while waiting for the urge to drop little atomic bombs into the lavatory.

"Since you don't read or do anything, what do you think of?" I asked some toilet-thinkers.

They stared at me as if I had just asked them how to breathe.

"What's there to think of? You just do it," they said incredulously.

Perhaps I should rethink that toilet-thinker moniker. Just-loo-it is rather apt, don't you think? Anyway, these folks are flabbergasted that some people can read despite the pong. They don't realise this is a non-issue for toilet-readers who can only smell the stink when the flush is hit.

I should know. I'm the type who have to grab something to read before I head for the loo. Anything which is at hand—yesterday's newspapers, last year's magazines or any book lying around would do. Undeniably people who read in the toilet have a habit of hogging the loo longer than necessary. It's always a case of "wait till I finish this article, page, chapter, or section before I grab the tissue" which could invariably take up a good half-hour or more.

I have a friend who reads the newspapers from front to back in the loo. Of course, it helps that his bathroom is very bright and spacious—as big as a walk-in wardrobe and it does not cramp his style to leisurely digest his daily.

Another friend grabs the encyclopaedia. It goes without saying that he's got the muscles to hold the heavy tome. He has a burly bouncer's build. If there's no reading material on hand, he'd take out his IC and driving license to "read". No kidding. Perhaps he's just admiring his mugshot.

When visiting another friend's house, I saw that she had pasted an envelope on the wall above the toilet-roll holder. Peeking out from the envelope were 3x5 cards of neatly written study notes for the part-time secretarial course she was pursuing while holding a full-time job. Being as hard-pressed for time as she was, this mother of one made full use of every minute of her time.

All this reading is fine and dandy if there's a clean toilet to use. If the stall is dirty, the only paper one needs in there is toilet paper. Here it's better to subscribe to the toilet-thinker's motto of just do it and scramble out real pronto.

Or one could take a leaf from my IC-reading friend. Whenever he has a big job to do while at work, he would drive three kilometres to a clean toilet as the loo at his workplace is dirty. Can't blame his colleagues for nicknaming him *"kam sze fatt"* (golden backside in Cantonese). Reminds me of the TV commercial which saw a man rushing home from the mall to his own fresh-smelling toilet.

Though I usually like to read something in the toilet, there's one exception to the rule. Well, two if I count filthy loos. A definite non-conducive environment for reading is a squatting toilet. I take my hats off to folks who can read while squatting. Imagine the multifarious skills at work here.

First, you got to squat and position the posterior accurately so as not to make a mess, then you have to shift the legs periodically to avoid pins and needles *and* hold up the reading material with one hand or two, if it's a newspaper. It's a Herculean task and not a very healthy one at that. I know someone who used to squat for hour-long sojourns in the toilet and the poor chap has haemorrhoids the size of grapes to show for them. (I know because it was described to me, not because I saw those "grapes", *eewww* ....) He's now cured of the malady and the marathon sessions, too.

Considering the large chunk of time people spend in the toilet, it's a matter of time before some bright spark comes up with a revolutionary idea on how to utilise that time wisely. That bright spark is none other than Microsoft. It was reported to be working on the iLoo which is a standard portable toilet with a wireless keyboard and extending, height-adjustable plasma screen in front of the seat. Users will be able to sit down, undock a wireless keyboard and conveniently access the first ever *www.c.com*. There was even talks of them linking up with toilet paper manufacturers to produce special web paper for those in need of URL inspiration. Sounds perfect for my IC-reading friend.

If these reports are true, I want the iLoo. Oh, I'll still be reading in the loo—when the power is down.

much ado over zits

ZITS have never been been a big cause of concern in my younger days. The occasional pimple did sprout up now and then but I never had a major outbreak. That is until I became pregnant with my first baby. The hormonal changes in my body caused an army of pimples to sprout up on my face and neck. The red lumps topped by white pus were unusually large and ripe for the picking.

Just looking at them made my hands itch. The protrusions seemed to be calling out, "Press me! Press me!" Despite well-meaning advice from others not to squeeze them, I couldn't keep my hands off them. I would stand really close to a full-length mirror and squeeze the zits out one by one. The pus hit the mirror with a squelch. By the time I was finished, the mirror was yellow polka-dotted.

As a result, my face looked as if it had miniature volcanoes all over it. When I distributed cakes at the office during the full moon celebration, one colleague asked me, "What happened to your face? You had chicken pox ah?" It was really that bad.

I'm glad that my "chicken pox" days are over but my children have yet to get over theirs. Children these days tend to mature at an earlier age. When my two older kids turned eleven, their faces took on the look of a pebble-strewn laterite road—red and uneven, especially at the forehead.

I couldn't keep my hands off their faces. I had to pop the pimples. Lying on the floor with their heads on my lap, I carefully place both thumbs around a pimple and press out the pus. If the pimple is ripe, sure enough the glob will come out. The emission usually comes out in two ways. If it's watery, it will shoot out water-pistol like. If it's dry, it will squirt out like toothpaste being squeezed out of a tube.

I stopped this habit when I stumbled upon this information in a medical encyclopaedia.

"It is dangerous to prick or squeeze a pimple about the upper lip, nose or cheeks as the blood and lymph channels from these areas drain directly into the skull at the base of the brain. Because of this anatomical structure, serious brain infections may sometimes result. Young people especially should be warned never to squeeze pimples or boils in these areas."

Whoa! Young people? Make that "mothers with itchy hands." From then on I steered clear of their faces but occasionally some ripe zits on their forehead would make me salivate.

Incidentally, zits can be conveniently used as a threat. "If you don't do as I say, I'm going to press that big pimple on your forehead!" It's enough to make the kids acquiesce, especially 12-year-old Yen Nee who had a particularly bad outbreak of acne. People kept commenting on her face and recommending various types of treatments.

"Try Cetaphil. It is very good," one friend recommended. So I bought Cetaphil from the pharmacy.

"You should try this dermatologically-tested soap. It is very effective. My son is using it and it works. I cut one third to use and keep the other two thirds so that it won't get dried up so quickly. But it's quite expensive, $75 a bar," another friend said. I bought a teensy-weensy one-third bar of soap from her for $25.

"You better do something about Yen Nee's face. It's so oily. Get her to bring a hanky or tissue to school to wipe her face with," my youngest brother advised me over the phone. I made sure she takes a pack of tissues to school.

"You must do something about Yen Nee's face before it gets worse," yet another friend implored. "Last time, I spent tens of thousands of dollars to treat my acne." Her voice broke as she remembered the anguish she went through during that trying period. "Buy *looi hu* for her to eat. This fish is very good for the skin." I tried to buy *looi hu* at the nearby market but it wasn't available.

Even my father-in-law had something to say. "What's wrong with Yen Nee's face?" he asked. Mum-in-law chipped in, "*Aiya*, you didn't tell me earlier. I would have brought some *bedak sejuk* (course granules of powder to be applied after mixing with water into a paste)."

All these comments made me more determined to put an end to her acne woes. In search of an effective acne-buster, I checked out every pharmacy I came across. I've lost track of the many different brands of facial cleansers I've bought for Yen Nee and her brother to use. Thankfully, the worst appears to be over. The acne on their faces have cleared up somewhat.

My nephew had it even worse. He had red patches of acne on his forehead and both cheeks. It was so bad that the doctor had to prescribe antibiotics for him. Then someone recommended a Chinese herb called *kim gin hua*, literally translated as golden silver flower. After taking the herb, to be brewed with boiling water like tea, there was some improvement. But the acne has yet to clear up completely. It looks like the teenager may have to drink potfuls of *kim gin hua* brew before he can see more skin than zits on his face.

I empathise with him and his mother. I've had my share of "chicken pox" days and worrying over my children's acne. I hope this malady would quickly end its biological run.

a matter of style

SOMEWHERE between my sweet-sixteen and twirling-twenties, I had this fixation with celebrities. Or to be more exact, their hairstyles which I liked to copy. When *Dallas* was the reigning soap opera in the 1980s, Victoria Principal's Pam Ewing character became a trend setter. I sported the same long straight hair which cascaded in layers around the face.

When Princess Diana shot to fame as Prince Charles' radiant bride, Princess Di's layered haircut was the rage of the day. Everywhere you turn, you can spot the familiar hairstyle.

I had never asked for a Demi Moore's *Ghost* hairstyle though I was told by hairstylists that it was a popular style when the movie was showing. Of course, those who copy celebrities' hairstyle don't just ape blindly. Just because their favourite star may sport a certain hairdo, they don't just jump onto the bandwagon. Otherwise, you would get scores of people walking around with *botak*-heads like Demi Moore's *GI Jane* character.

As the candles on my birthday cake increase, my propensity to copy superstar's hairstyles decreased. Having said that, the hairstyles I used to copy were decent-looking, never outrageous like Cindy Lauper's, nor flamboyant like Farrah Fawcett's tawny mane.

Later I resorted to hairstyle magazines to choose a style. I'm not like some people who can stick with the same style year after year just because that particular style suits them. I like variety, within boundaries of course. I would walk into the saloon, grab a hair magazine, flip through the pages, identify the hairstyle I want and point it out to the hairdresser, "There! I want to look like that."

Of course, the likelihood of me getting the exact hairstyle as the model is as remote as the possibility of me being the next Bond girl. For the life of me, I can't understand how I could get Pam Ewing and Princess Di's hairstyles but not one which stares out of the pages of a hair magazine. Perhaps having the picture right there for comparison raises the expectation a notch too high.

Inevitably I would end up being disappointed with the result. There are two possible reasons for that. For starters, the hairdresser may not have the skill to recreate that particular style. Secondly, my hair may not have the necessary length, texture or volume to carry that style. If the hairdresser is honest, she'll tell me the truth. Otherwise, I'll just have to discover the plain (or ugly) truth for myself later.

Throughout the years, I've learnt to adjust my expectation. I don't expect hairdressers to be magicians anymore. I'm happy if my hair does not end up too curly like Phua Chu Kang's, or too flat like his sister-in-law's.

Though variety is the spice of life, my type of spice is of the black variety as far as hair colour is concerned. Despite hairdressers persuading me to jazz up my hair by highlighting or colouring it, I've staunchly stood my ground. I like my black hair though one effeminate hairdresser taunted me with "You think your hair is very black-*meh?*" Excuse me, sir. Though my hair is not silky raven black like shampoo models', it's blacker than others' and that's good enough for me.

Admittedly I may change my mind in future. I've spotted stray strands of white hair on my head. The day will come when more white strands will invade the black territory. That's when I'll consider dyeing my hair. And it would be a dark brown colour to match my tanned skin. Not the blond or garish vermilion (honest!) that I've seen on some young and not-so-young people.

Some folks just don't get it. We don't have the complexion to wear blond hair, though those who are very fair may get away with it. Forget the vermilion! Even Caucasians don't have that hair colour unless it's on Bozo the clown.

As for me, I'll play it safe by sticking to the staid.

CHEERS AND JEERS

it's a spectator sport all right

I HAVE watched enough football matches to last me a lifetime. I was merely performing my wifely duty by staying up with hubby to watch live games till the wee hours of the morning.

Thankfully, my firstborn came along and I was spared this boring, sleep inducing game when he became old enough to appreciate this spectator sport. I tell my boy that once he's seen a game, he's seen them all.

It's really amazing, this football. It's the common bond that unites everyone, whether one is president of a country, executive or newspaper vendor. You see them glued to their TV screens, watching 22 grown men scrambling for a ball. If an alien from outer space were to land on a football field during a match, it would laugh at their idiocy and tell them to each get his own ball.

Now the World Cup fever is on. I can hear shouts of "GOAL!" every night—from the boys in the family, from the neighbours and from the *roti canai* stall behind my house.

One night, I heard a chorus of "Wow ... Wow ... WOWWW!" from the *roti canai* stall. I don't have to be Sherlock Holmes to guess what happened. First attempt to shoot, blocked; second try, foiled; third kick, GOAL! Elementary, my dear Watson, elementary.

Anyway, to get back to the point: after you have seen one game, you've seen them all, except who wins the match. The behaviour and quirks of players, officials and fans are the same everywhere.

When a player gets a chance to shoot, observe carefully. You're about to see drama in action. He strikes. Camera zooms in on face of player. Expectancy ... is it in or is it out? If it's a miss, agony is written all over his face.

If the ball enters the net, the crowd will be up on their feet with a deafening roar. You'll see the goal-scorer tearing down the field like a charging cheetah. Hands will grab him, but he'd brush them off and continue to yell and pump his fists. Jubilation! That's what sports writers like to write.

Sometimes, he'd pull off his shirt. Don't ask me why. Maybe he wants fans to admire the torso attached to those legs that slammed the ball into the goalmouth.

Other times, at the end of the run, he may land on his knees with tears flowing down his cheeks. Amazing how emotional a man can be, weeping like a baby over a goal.

Then, his teammates will start jumping on him, hugging him or kissing him. This, from some men who wouldn't touch another of their own gender under other circumstances.

If you want to see a Michael Jackson act—you know, the crotch-grabbing one, watch out for the free kicks. Players line up in front of the goalmouth. Hands in *that* position before the ball flies. Gotta protect the family jewels to ensure a future generation. I suspect players don't like free kicks awarded to opponents not only for the obvious reason but also because of the embarrassing stance they have to assume.

The guy who sounds and acts like a traffic cop is the referee. Perennially, one hand would be on the whistle, other hand raised, either horizontally or vertically. Peeet! Foul! Peeet! Yellow card! Peeet! Red card! Peeet! Half time. Peeet! Game over. What a relief it must be for his poor ears when it's time to hit the showers. I wonder if he wears earplugs? The whistle could be an occupational hazard for football referees.

The team manager is usually with the substitutes at the sidelines. It's easy to recognise him. He may be sitting down on the bench with elbows resting on knees, looking like his house has just been burnt down. Or he'd be bouncing on his feet, like he had just won the lottery. It depends on how well or badly his team is playing.

Sometimes, you'll see him pacing up and down the sidelines, as if waiting outside the delivery room while his wife is in labour. At other times, he may be chewing gum furiously or yelling at his players. The TV never lets us hear what he's saying. As a novice, I can only conjecture. "Strike! Strike! Defend! Defend! Mark him! Mark him!"

As with any spectator sport. a game wouldn't be complete without the fans. They range from the sexy to unusual. Sports photographers like to shoot attractive female fans garbed in tight fitting or revealing attire. Never mind the action, such photos will sell for sure.

Then there are fans who paint their faces like Native American braves. Their team colours splashed across their cheeks and national flag draped around their shoulders like a poncho, this breed looks like they're going to war.

Whatever their garb may be, if there's a goal, there's a howl. But whether of joy or anguish, it depends on which side that scores.

cheers to the cup

MY HUSBAND is crazy over badminton. He must play his weekly games or he would feel like a fish out of water.

If the hall where he regularly plays is booked for other functions, he would drive all the way from Klang to Kuala Lumpur where his folks could book a court at the condo where they live, just so he can play badminton.

I have to schedule our timetable around his badminton so that they do not clash. Otherwise, it goes without saying which activity would get the boot.

Oh, I play badminton too. Like once every five years. The following day would invariably see me bent double with back pain, joint pain and what-have-you as a result of rusty muscles being coerced into accelerated action.

Yet when it comes to cheering for the Malaysian team at the Thomas Cup, my husband the badminton aficionado sits relaxed on the sofa with hands behind his head while I jump up and down like a monkey and hurl cushions onto the floor.

It doesn't make sense at all.

Take the semi-finals between Malaysia and China. In the nail-biting clash between Mohd Hafiz and Bao Chunlai, I was almost tearing my hair out in excitement. Whenever Hafiz scored a point, I would shout "Yes! Yes!" in jubilation. When he was at game point, I would repeatedly exhort "Come on! Come on! Come on! End it now! End it now!".

My eleven-month old baby learnt that it was not conducive to be playing near a vociferous mummy when Thomas Cup fever is in the air. At one point I startled her with my shouting. While changing her nappy later, I gesticulated wildly with an open safety pin in one hand.

I caught her eyeing me with a fascinated smile. She must have been thinking, "There's something wrong with my mummy."

Hafiz eventually won the match. I leaped like a trampoline jumper while my husband the realist remarked, "We have not won the cup yet-*lah*." Killjoy.

When our second doubles pair fought back from the brink of defeat to take Malaysia into the finals, I jumped for joy with a "Yeah! Yeah! Yeah!" while my husband the cool spectator looked on amusedly.

It was even more electrifying in the finals. With young Lee Tsuen Seng playing his guts out against Indonesia's Taufik Hidayat, my support became noisier. I didn't realise how loud my screams were until I saw my children running down the stairs to investigate the ruckus.

"What's happening?" one asked.

"What's wrong, mummy?" from another.

"Mummy is winning the Thomas Cup," my husband replied.

Really, BAM should consider appointing me as their chief cheerleader.

With Tsuen Seng clinching another point for Malaysia, we were leading 2-1! I could hardly believe it. The Thomas Cup was within our reach!

I don't remember expending so much emotional energy into cheering the Malaysian badminton team. The last time was probably in 1992 when we last won the cup. Please, let us win it again. Ten years is a long enough wait.

When Lee Wan Wah and Choong Tan Fook took to the courts, all Malaysians must be hoping that they could make it a 3-1 victory for Malaysia. The situation was extremely volatile. In an agonising moment, I smashed my hands down on the table to which my daughter admonished, "Mummy ah!" Mother-daughter role had been reversed.

I also sounded like a broken record with "Gone-*lah*, gone-*lah*, gone-*lah*, gone-*lah*" whenever the opponents smashed our players repeatedly. On the other hand, my husband the badminton coach would give me a crash course on the intricacies of badminton tactics.

"You see in badminton, when you keep on smashing and the opponents could return your smash, you feel very demoralised. But if you could kill the smash, wah, you feel very motivated."

I continued to moan and groan when our players kept losing points. I despaired at the look of desperation on their faces each time their opponents wrest the service from them. The Indonesian doubles pair managed to level the score to 2-2.

The four matches thus far had delivered adrenalin-pumping action. Alternating between euphoria and despair, hope and trepidation, my heart was going bip-bop bip-bop bip-bop. It was more thrilling than watching a suspense movie.

As the fifth match progressed, I could feel my enthusiasm waning. While I *aiya*-ed and *aiyo*-ed at

Indonesia's steady advancement, my husband the
badminton pundit was analysing the Malaysian player's
performance. "I don't think he can win. He's too
inconsistent. He's not varying his play. He's not playing
enough corners. He's hitting the shuttle directly to the
opponent."

True enough, Malaysia lost the last match and with
that the Thomas Cup slipped from our grasp, yet again.
Sigh and double sigh.

My husband the badminton player didn't wait to see
Indonesia celebrate their win. He was off to get his weekly
badminton fix which is more addictive and exciting than
the Thomas Cup.

so what's the big deal?

"**A**T LAST! World Cup is here after four years," football fans say.

"Alas! World Cup is here again!?" I say with dismay.

Everywhere I turn, I'm bombarded with images of the golden World Cup trophy and footballers in striking poses. For starters, my newspaper weighs more due to its 16-page daily pull-out. Then there's the hype on television, over the radio, on the Internet, on the highways and byways. There's just no end to this madness.

What else do you call this fever which rages and afflicts a wide plethora of people, from presidents to students, office workers to refuse collectors, vicars to homemakers. Oh, wait a minute, I seem to forget a new word which has been coined for it: footballitis.

Yes, that's the sickness which manifests its symptom in rearranging the priorities of denizens around the world. One case in point is England where some churches have changed their service times to accommodate the World Cup matches. An archbishop was quoted as saying "Worship comes first, of course, but this comes round only every four years so we can afford to be flexible."

In football-crazed Brazil, its President has changed the working hours of civil servants to start at midday so that they don't have to miss out on the World Cup action. Instead of working from 10 to five, they work from noon to seven. I won't be surprised if the Brazilian civil sector sees a surge in job applications after this.

Closer home, I heard that a friend's husband has taken a television set to his office. Furthermore, he is arranging business appointments around the football matches so that he doesn't have to miss a game. If all football fans were self-employed, the economy would surely grind to a halt.

Our television stations have really outdone themselves this time. Not one, mind you, but all three stations are carrying live telecasts. It's pure bliss for football maniacs but absolute misery for non-fans.

You can't watch any programme without it being frequently punctuated by World Cup commercials. I'm not a couch potato so it doesn't matter that regular programmes are being preempted for live broadcasts. What is exasperating is that for the few programmes that I choose to watch, I don't get to watch them because of one football enthusiast in the family.

Take the opening day of the World Cup. The match between France and Senegal started at 7.30p.m. but as we had to go for church service (unlike the English, we still have our priorities right), my husband recorded the match on tape.

When we came home, it was a tussle for the television. Hubby couldn't wait to play the tape of the game. My son wanted to watch *WWE* while my daughter and I was hoping to see *Charmed*.

"Daddy, why don't you watch the tape tomorrow? Mummy can see *Charmed* while I can tape up *WWE*," my son suggested.

A win-win solution, if I may say.

"No," said his father who has already begun to play the tape.

"But Triple H is wrestling tonight!"

"It's all pretend. No need to see *WWE*."

My son should have known he couldn't win this battle. His father's staple television diet is football programmes: this league or that league or football highlights. Now we're talking of the grandmother of all football shows which only comes once in four years.

Son, it's easier for you to earn your own money and buy your own television set than for your dad to give up the remote control during World Cup season.

No *Charmed*, no *WWE*. So we sat down and watched the match. After five minutes, I yawned. I didn't bother to stifle it. I yawned widely and loudly. What were they thinking of when they called this the "greatest show on Earth"? I'm telling you it's one big yawn. No, make that many big yawns.

"So boring," I said. "Why don't you fast forward the tape to the end so you'll know who won the match."

Of course, hubby pooh-poohed the idea. You know, all that stuff about watching the action, not just knowing the score.

My neighbours have been infected with an even more severe case of footballitis. The other day I was cooking dinner when I heard a piercing shriek. It was my neighbour's 13-year-old son. He continued screaming for a minute or so. His sister, who was in the kitchen, responded by asking "Japan goal-*ah*?" before she rushed out to the living room to catch the excitement and replay.

At night when the man of the house returns from work, there'd be a symphony of cheers whenever a goal is scored, ranging from the children's soprano to the father's guttural bass.

I'm counting the days till the Final.

CHOW TIME

it's a wrap!

Y OU can't learn how to wrap rice dumplings from a recipe book. How do you "fold over a bamboo leaf to cover the rice to form a triangle-shaped dumpling"? And how about "securing a string around the dumpling" when you don't know which side of the triangle should be tied?

Well-written recipes can yield wonderful results even for novice cooks but when it comes to wrapping *chang* (rice dumpling), no amount of precise instructions can take the place of hands-on coaching.

So I ended up in mum's kitchen trying to learn the intricacies of *chang*-wrapping from her. She had prepared all the necessary ingredients: glutinous rice fried with black eye beans, pork, split green beans, chestnuts and mushrooms.

She took two pieces of bamboo leaves from the pail where they had been soaked overnight. She overlapped the leaves and folded them into a cone. One scoop of rice, a spoon of green beans, and a piece each of chestnut, mushroom and pork followed by another big scoop of rice. She compacted the ingredients with the back of a spoon. With deft fingers, she closed up the cone and folded up the leaves into the shape of a pyramid. Then she took a hemp string and tied it around the middle.

The first two steps were simple enough. The problematic part was shaping it into a pyramid. The bamboo leaves just refused to cooperate. They wouldn't let me mould them into a nice little pyramid. A bad workman blames his tools, I know. After struggling for a while, I finally handed it over to mum to finish the job. With a press here and a tuck there, she produced a perfect little pyramid.

The next step—tying the string around the *chang*—was just as challenging. If it was tied the wrong way, the string would slip during the cooking process and the dumpling would go out of shape. If this was the case, it's better for it to be so badly tied that it'd slip when being transferred to the pot so that the mistake can be rectified before it lands into hot water, literally and figuratively.

I was a slow learner. In one hour, I managed to wrap a grand total of 12 *changs*. If this were a race, even Mr. Tortoise would beat me. Nonetheless, I felt a sense of achievement for having successfully tied a few bundles of dumplings and went round distributing some to friends. I didn't tell my friends I "made" the dumplings. That would have been claiming all the credit for myself when I didn't do all the work. I said, "I helped my mum wrap them."

That was last year. This year I took the plunge and did everything on my own without mum's help except for SOS phone calls.

I bought and prepared all the necessary ingredients: bamboo leaves, hemp string, glutinous rice, pork, beans and mushrooms. I'm always looking for shortcuts so I decided to use minced meat to avoid having to cut it up into bite-sized chunks. Besides I don't fancy eating stringy meat which I've so often eaten in rice dumplings when they were not well cooked. I left out the chestnuts as my kids don't like them. Less filling means smaller dumplings that are easier to handle.

I started work at 10.30a.m. By the time I wrapped it up (pardon the pun!), it was 7.00p.m. Though I had two breaks in between, one to fetch my daughter from school and the other to watch my favourite Korean drama, my shoulders felt as if a 10kg bag of rice was resting on them. Now I understood why my mum complained of backache when she was making *chang* the other day.

Out of 120 *changs*, only two came loose. Not bad for a beginner. That's about the only good thing I can say about my first dumpling-making experience. Instead of sporting pointy ends, the *changs* had a dog-eared look not unlike origami animal heads. Some have grooves on the surface. Others had an additional ridge at the bottom of the pyramid due to the rice not being tucked in properly. Instead of a bright yellow, the sweet dumplings were pale as I used too little alkaline water.

The savoury dumplings were not salty enough. They were short on black soya sauce, five-spice powder and salt. If I were in a cooking school, I would have gotten an F. Their only redeeming quality is that they were well-cooked and tender.

That night we had *chang* for dinner. I had warned hubby that they were rather bland, so he didn't comment on the taste. Instead he asked, "Where's the meat?" The irony was not lost on me. This was supposed to be a *bak chang* (meat dumpling), but the meat could not be seen or tasted.

I explained my rationale for using minced meat. He gave me a withering look and proceeded to eat six more *changs* (these were size "S" dumplings). He had no choice— there wasn't any other food for dinner. Though he's not a fussy eater, out came the tomato and chilli sauce to enhance the flavour of the bland *chang*.

The *changs* were not fit to be distributed but I still had to fulfill my obligation to family members. Next time, I'll give them something better to chew on. I just have to get the *changs* to shape up and, more importantly, to get the taste right. It's time to look for recipes.

a potful of leaping flavours

I WAS STRIDING quickly past the Chinese herbs and vegetables in a morning market one day when I came across frog meat already cleaned and arranged neatly on an overturned blue basket.

Memories of piping frog porridge eaten on cold rainy nights came rushing back. Years ago, when some of my uncles lived in the same neighbourhood as us, they would get together to catch frogs on rainy days. Armed with long-poled nets and plastic bags, they sought out drains and waterlogged areas for the croakers.

While waiting for the main ingredient to be caught, mum would cook the porridge. My uncles always returned with a big catch. They dumped the live frogs onto the porch floor and proceeded to slaughter them under the running tap. I never saw how they did it as they were all hunched over the frogs, not that I was interested, anyway.

After the frogs were dressed and cut up into small pieces, mum would take over.

After all the preparations had been made mum placed the meat into the porridge together with shredded ginger. If the catch was plentiful, she would cook an additional dish of stir-fried frogs with dark soya sauce and dried chillies.

Having changed into dry clothes, my uncles would be ready for their reward—delicious frog porridge served steaming hot.

Looking at the frogs on the blue basket, I could almost see the steam curling up from the porridge they would be swimming in later. I decided to buy the frog meat, paying ten ringgit for four pieces. Then I stopped at the *kuih* (local cakes) stall to buy four pieces of *yew char koay* (deep-fried strips of dough) as a side dish.

I have cooked chicken porridge, pork porridge and fish porridge before but not frog porridge. To be on the safe side, I rang mum to ask her how to clean the frogs and cook the dish.

"Pull out the veins from the legs," mum instructed.

"What about the black stain near the stomach?" I asked.

"Clean it off, then cut the frog into small pieces. Cook the porridge first. Add the frog pieces at the end so that the meat won't be so tough. Then season with *kicap* (soya sauce), salt, pepper and sesame oil. Don't forget the ginger," she said.

I saw something which looked like a vein but couldn't pull it out as easily as mum said it would come off. Then I tried to clean off the black stuff but it couldn't be removed easily either. If I were to scrape it off, by the time I was done, half the meat would have gone down the drain. So I just let it be.

I boiled the porridge for about half an hour. As I was about to add the frog pieces and seasoning, I noticed that the broth was rather thick and so I added more water and brought it to a boil before adding the meat and seasoning.

That evening we had frog porridge for dinner. As we had to go to church that night, the younger children and I ate first as hubby would return quite late after picking up Tze Wei from afternoon school. I didn't tell the children what porridge they were eating, knowing that it might freak them out if they knew what it was. They polished up their plates quickly though porridge wasn't their favourite food. The *yew char koay* helped it go down faster.

When Tze Wei and his father returned, as usual the 13-year-old asked, "What's for dinner?"

His father had taken a look at the dish and knew what it was.

"Frog porridge," he answered.

"Eeeww! Frog porridge! I don't want to eat it!" he screamed. But being the culinary adventurer that he is, he tucked in heartily.

I still haven't told the younger kids they have eaten something which went "Croak! Croak!" but then again, I believe that sometimes ignorance is bliss.

one girl's meat,
another boy's poison

COOKING for a family of six can be a challenging task considering the different tastebuds of each family member.

My 13-year-old son Tze Wei likes to eat curry. The aroma of curry and *rendang* cooked by our Malay neighbour always waft over to our house. As soon as he gets a whiff of curry, he would come sniffing around the kitchen like a cartoon character following a thick trail of aroma and asks, "Is that the smell of your cooking?" More often than not, he has to walk away disappointed.

You see, I hardly cook spicy food as 12-year-old Yen Nee and six-year-old Tze Ren can't handle hot stuff. At least the little guy is more sporting in trying out a little chilli occasionally but his sister can't tolerate even a teensy-weensy bit of chilli, not even the mild-tasting *dhall* curry which comes with *roti canai*.

So if we're having spicy fried fish for dinner, I have to cook one plain for Yen Nee. If I prepare curry chicken, I have to make sure two other dishes are to her liking. Otherwise, she might end up eating rice with gravy only.

Even though we came up with a hotness ranking system to help her spice up her culinary experience, she hasn't taken to it. The ranking ranged from 1 for mild to 10 for sizzling hot. We would tell her, "Try this curry. It's a 2." She would dip the tip of her spoon into the curry, taste it tentatively and yell, "It's very hot! It's not a 2, it's a 10!" and quickly gulp down a cup of water.

Tze Wei is more adventurous in his food intake, taking beef, lamb and venison in his stride. He has even acquired the taste of eating raw garlic in light soya sauce after seeing my grandma enjoying it with her Hokkien mee. His tastebuds can jump into overdrive—he once ate chocolate cake with *assam* fish gravy!

But there's something Tze Wei wouldn't touch—*mee boon kueh*, a Hokkien dish of small dough pieces cooked in *ikan bilis* soup. His father doesn't like it either, though he will eat it if he has no choice.

I used to detest *mee boon kueh* but when I was pregnant with Yen Nee, I developed a craving for it. That could explain why she likes to eat this soupy concoction.

Tze Ren doesn't like soft and mushy food like tofu or steamed egg. But then again his taste can be eclectic. He loves Japanese jelly but not *agar-agar* (local jelly). He enjoys red bean dumpling but refuses to eat the *kaya* bun. He hates vegetables. A thin sliver of cabbage or onion is enough to make him gag.

Tze Wei and Yen Nee refused to eat vegetables when they were younger too. It's only when they were older that we twisted their arms to make them eat their greens. Nowadays, they're always complaining, "You made us eat vegetables when we were six. Now it's time for Tze Ren to learn to eat vegetables. Don't give him anything except vegetables." How I envy my sister-in-law for her daughters who love to chomp on raw lettuce.

The older children have now acquired the habit of eating vegetables although they will eat them grudgingly if it's not their favourite. Yen Nee likes long beans, broccoli and cauliflower, while Tze Wei prefers beansprouts and stir-fried spinach. If I cook spinach soup, he would grumble but Yen Nee loves it.

So we take turns. If it's spinach soup this time, it'd be stir-fried next. It's the same for favourite food. I can't prepare everybody's favourite chow all the time. But sometimes all it takes is a little improvising to please everybody. We all love garlic bread except Yen Nee. So I would prepare a few pieces without garlic so that she gets to eat "garlic bread" sans garlic.

Two-year-old Su Yen is experimenting with all kinds of new food and to her everything is good, except porridge. She must have gotten so sick of it when I served it for her lunch and dinner for months on end. Now she's eating the same food as the rest of the family, which is good for both of us as she gets to enjoy a wider variety of food and I don't have to cook porridge just for her.

The only food that all the children enjoy is fast food. Trips to McDonald's, KFC or Pizza Hut are eagerly anticipated. The two younger ones in particular would be on cloud nine if the restaurant has a playground for them to romp in.

Fortunately, my husband is not choosy about food. He can eat anything I dish out. Once I cooked Cantonese-style noodles in an egg-based sauce which turned out too thick as I had been too liberal with the starch. The result was unappetising—the noodles looked like strips of papier-mache in glue. I couldn't stomach the food and had to chuck it halfway but he wiped his plate clean.

Having four children with a wide array of culinary likes and dislikes, it's a blessing to have a husband whose attitude is "food is food," and is edible, no matter how yucky.

burpy days are here again!

HAVE you ever wondered how the durian came about? There is a tale from the Philippines about the fruit. It tells the ancient story of a powerful king from the Philippines who is sad because he is ignored by his young wife. He consults a wise hermit who tells him the way to plant a special tree to win her heart. The king follows this advice and with the help of a nymph of the air wins his wife's heart. The king holds a big celebration but the wise hermit is somehow not invited. Angry, the hermit curses the special tree to produce a fruit called the durian.

If this tale is true, then we should thank the wise hermit. The durian is so highly regarded by Malaysians that we call it the king of fruits. Whenever it is in season, durian lovers smack their lips with anticipation while the small percentage of durian haters scurry for olfactory cover.

I belong to the former category and like any true-blue Malaysian, I can tell you the best way durians should be eaten—straight from the husk, not from a styrofoam packet bought from the supermarket or from a Tupperware in which to *ta pau* (take away) the succulent morsels from the roadside vendor.

Nothing beats huddling around a cluster of durians, waiting with drooling saliva for the appointed durian opener to split the thorny husk, then wolfing down the custard-like morsels faster than it takes to open the fruit. Or in Manglish: Best!

Really, it's no fun eating durians alone. They should be enjoyed en masse. The more hands jostling for choice morsels, the more enjoyable the experience, provided there's enough to go round for everyone.

Which brings me to my next observation. Durians have an addictive quality that induces you to eat until fully gratified. If there aren't enough to satiate the palate, you're bound to come away feeling dissatisfied and craving for more. It's not like eating apples. You get one slice and that's fine, you won't hanker for more. With durians, you taste one morsel and you want a dozen more.

It's undeniable that the durian is the king of fruits in Malaysia. It's the only fruit that can hold its own. Haven't we all been to durian parties where the menu is durians, durians and more durians? Tell me, have you heard of a papaya party or a mangosteen party even? Of course, you haven't, unless you count orange-throwing during Chap Goh Meh as a fruit party.

In fact, my most memorable durian-eating experience was at durian parties where the luscious fruits were aplenty and don't cost me a single cent.

My ex-employer used to organise such parties at his house where staff members and their families get to gorge on durians by the truckloads. I enjoyed those fiestas—where else would I get to eat all the D24s to my heart's content without denting the bank balance?

My husband's boss did something a little different. He invited employees to his durian orchard in a neighbouring state. He didn't show up for the trip but his adolescent son and chauffeur led a convoy of half a dozen cars to the orchard.

We made our way to a little hut in the middle of the plantation. The caretaker had already collected a huge basket of durians for us. There, on the bare cement floor of the ramshackle hut, durians were opened for our feasting. We even *ta pau*-ed some home.

There was another occasion when a friend had bought a big basket (the type used by wholesale fruit vendors) of durians, too much for his family of five to consume. He invited church members to drop by his house to savour the durians after evening Bible class. We didn't even enter the house. We dug in right there on the porch. We came, we ate, we left. Just like that.

Although I love to eat durians, I'm hopeless when it comes to buying them. Usually I let the vendor choose the best fruits and threaten to return them if they are no good. Works most of the time. I admire those who pick up a durian, hold it close to their ear and shake it. They know what to look for. I don't. So I asked a friend who is something of a durian expert on how to choose good durians.

"When you shake the durian and you hear a rocking sound, that's good. It means the flesh is firm and not soggy. Choose durians that are light. A heavy durian means more moisture in the durian and thicker husks which could mean smaller morsels," he said.

Another point worthy of mention is the practice of drinking salt water from the husk after consuming the fruits. It is supposed to counter the "heaty" (*yang*) effects of too much durians. (I'm not sure if this is proven but it does no harm unless you accidentally poke yourself with the thorns.)

That's why you should eat durians straight from the husk. Can you imagine drinking salt water from a styrofoam tray? It doesn't have any "magical cooling properties" and it's difficult to balance the tray of water without spilling it.

Eating durians may be fun but dealing with the after-effects isn't. During durian season, you'd better be wary when confined in enclosed spaces such as lifts. You will know when you are in the presence of someone who has taken too much durians. He might just release a stink bomb via the nether regions of his anatomy. You'd better get out at the next floor or be prepared to hold your breath till you turn blue.

The toilet is another place where you may have to breathe through your mouth when you need to ease yourself after bingeing on durians. After undergoing the digestion process, the aroma of durians is transformed into the smell of rotten eggs.

So perhaps we should be more sympathetic to Mat Sallehs who think our beloved fruit smells like rotting fruit in a blocked drain. Some people even regard this spiky-shelled pungent fruit as "skunk of the orchards" and the stinkiest fruit on the planet. Is it any wonder then that durians are banned from hotels and other public places and on buses, trains and planes across Southeast Asia?

mooning over mooncakes

T HE Mid-Autumn Festival is mooncake galore season. From as early as two months before the actual date of the festival, bakeries and little carts set up in shopping malls have started to offer a tempting array of mooncakes.

But their astronomical prices make me think twice before splurging on these delicacies. Perhaps the only thing that's worthwhile about these pricey purchases is the beautiful box they come in. Whether made of cardboard, tin or wood, these receptacles are good enough to be keepsakes.

There are three alternatives for mooncake lovers – pay up, buy the cheap plastic-wrapped variety but be prepared to choke on its dryness or make your own.

Feeling adventurous, I chose the third option. I enlisted the help of a friend whom I shall call *Sifu* (Cantonese for 'Master') who had learnt the technique of making mooncakes the previous year. Though she wasn't confident enough to give me a hands-on lesson, she passed me the recipe with some pointers and lent me her mooncake mould.

After sitting on the recipe for two weeks, I finally got things going and bought the ingredients from a specialty bakery shop. There was an assortment of precooked mooncake filling available—lotus, plain or with durian, green tea or *pandan* flavoured, red bean paste and even chocolate-flavoured paste. *Sifu* advised me to start with the cheapest variety—red bean—so that cost can be minimised in case of failure.

I procrastinated some more until *Sifu* rang me to give me a modified recipe which she said yielded satisfactory results. Realising that she'd be flying off to South Korea that night for a holiday, I quickly swung into action in case I needed to SOS her for help.

First I made the dough for the skin. I mixed the Hongkong *pau* flour, golden syrup, peanut oil and alkaline water into a sticky paste. It had to stand for four hours to make it easier to handle.

Later I roasted some melon seeds in the oven for five minutes till they popped and added them to the red bean paste. As there were lots of seeds, the paste was a tad too prickly to knead out evenly.

I weighed the individual portions of skin and filling as instructed by *Sifu* earlier. Looking at the dough and filling that were like a ping pong and tennis ball respectively, I thought *Sifu* had made a mistake.

Time for an SOS call.

"Are you sure you gave me the right proportion of dough to filling? The dough is too little to cover the filling."

"It's correct," *Sifu* insisted. "You have to spread out the dough on your palm, put the filling in, then slowly wrap it upwards."

Sounded simple enough, but I discovered it was easier said than done. I pressed the dough flat and held it up.

It was so stretchy that gravity tore a hole in the middle. Looked like I had a tough task at hand. Wrapping that tiny blob of dough around the big ball of filling was more difficult than squeezing myself into clothes two sizes too small.

After some rubbing, pulling and stretching and patchworks here and there, I finally managed to clothe the paste with the skin. I dropped the ball into the mould that had been lightly dusted with flour and pressed it in snugly. It was such a tight fit that when I tried to knock it out, it wouldn't dislodge.

A banging party ensued. I thumped the mould so hard on the table that I woke up my toddler who was napping.

It was still stuck.

I took a pestle and pounded the back of the mould. It refused to budge. It must have been over a hundred thwacks later that the mooncake *slowly* dropped out of the mould. The beautiful motif was utterly ruined. The dough stood out in little peaks where it had been separated reluctantly from the mould which had remnants still stuck to it. My brother later said that the mooncake looked like an acid-maimed face.

But practice makes perfect. As work progressed, the wrapping and demoulding became easier. I delegated the knocking to my six-year-old son who did a pretty good job, though some pieces looked like the Leaning Tower of Pisa after they landed on their sides.

When it was time to bake the mooncakes, I realised that I had forgotten to ask *Sifu* how to get rid of the excess flour from the mooncake surface. It was too late to call her as she was on her way to South Korea.

Sigh, I'll just have to do what I can. I tried to dust off as much flour as possible without disfiguring the mooncake further. Then I popped them into the oven. *Que Sera Sera, what will be, will be.* Fortunately, the egg-wash midway through baking took care of the flour problem.

The mooncakes turned out okay. They're not pretty but edible. My sister's verdict was kinder than my brother's. She said, "Not bad."

Thank you, Sifu!

what to eat next?

"DO you still eat chicken?" my mother-in-law asked me last weekend.

"Yes, but less," I replied.

"Better not to eat it," my father-in-law said.

A week earlier, my mother had said: "I went to the *pasar malam* to buy chicken but there's none. Both chicken sellers didn't turn up as there's no business."

Such conversations are probably echoing throughout Malaysia, nay, across Asia where bird flu has made its presence felt, either directly or indirectly.

Millions of chickens have been culled in 10 Asian countries, among them Thailand and Vietnam where the disease has claimed more than 20 lives. Most of the cases have been traced to direct contact with sick birds. Although there hasn't been any reported incidence of virus transmission during the preparation and consumption of chicken, people prefer to err on the side of caution.

Everywhere politicians assure their people that chicken is safe for consumption by eating chicken publicly. Interested parties organise eat-chicken campaigns to spur demand for poultry. (When free chicken meals are offered, chicken phobia is forgotten and the meals would be snapped up faster than you can say, "Squawk!")

The Malaysian government has banned the import of poultry from Thailand and given the assurance that locally reared poultry is safe. However, that hasn't stop the demand from declining. As a result, the price of poultry has gone down.

Some hypermarkets have put up large signs proclaiming: "Our poultry is locally produced." But their chicken is not fresh. I bought some chicken fillet the other day and discovered that they stank after I removed the cling wrap at home. I cooked them for the dogs. The dogs are still alive.

Poultry producers have taken out full-page press advertisements proclaiming that their fowls are raised locally and go through strict quality control. Food outlets have modified their menus to reduce the number of chicken dishes and increase dishes cooked with other meats.

The bird flu virus is not the only virus that has ramifications on what we serve on the dining table. There are other deadly viruses which infect livestock and people, which can bring entire industries to their knees. And they seem to be taking turns in afflicting different livestock.

In 2003, China carried out massive culling operations of civet cats, cooked as a delicacy, to stem the spread of Severe Acute Respiratory Syndrome (SARS) which killed 916 people worldwide. As the virus surfaced again in January 2004 after a man in the Guangdong province was confirmed to have contracted SARS, it was announced that another 10,000 civet cats would be slaughtered. These culling exercises may not impact the food-supply system. After all, how many can afford the dragon-tiger-phoenix soup consisting of snake, civet cat and chicken, or indeed can stomach such an exotic dish? But there are other concerns, such as the transmission of the disease during the culling process and driving the civet cat trade underground which could be counter-productive.

Three years earlier, it was the mad cow disease that wreaked havoc in several European countries. Malaysia banned the import of cattle and beef from some European countries to prevent the spread of the disease here. Understandably, people felt jittery about consuming beef.

Further back, in 1998, it was the pigs' turn. The Nipah virus that caused the so-called J.E. outbreak claimed the lives of 106 pig farmers and workers. The virus spread through direct contact with infected pigs. Though there wasn't any reason to believe that the virus could spread through the preparation and consumption of pork, people decided to play safe. That meant no pork in the diet. Pig farmers and porksellers were hard hit.

First pork. Then beef. Now chicken. The bird flu is affecting more people's diet than the Nipah virus and mad cow disease as Muslims don't eat pork and Hindus don't take beef. But most people eat chicken except vegetarians who are spared these "meaty" issues. What they have to worry about is the excessive use of pesticide on vegetables and fruits.

What next? Mutton? Seafood? So far there hasn't been any widespread scourge afflicting sheep. Hopefully there will not be. In the case of seafood, concerns are floating around regarding the excessive use of preservatives to keep the catch fresh during the journey from sea to land and from fishermen to retailers. We may have to find a better way than looking for firm flesh and red gills to indicate the freshness of fish. How can we tell if it has soaked up excessive chemicals?

As it is, housewives are wont to lament to one other at the market: "Don't know what to cook-*lah!*" This rhetorical question may be prompted by the desire for variety. And these food scares—rightly or wrongly—are not helping at all. At the end of the day, I think a reasoning mind and an everything-in-moderation credo will help answer the question of what to eat.

But don't ever ask Cambodians that question as they may suggest "spicy fried rat meat." If you think rats are dirty vermins or they remind you of *Fear Factor* challenges of gobbling up yucky stuff like sheep brain, raw pig liver or rare rat steak, just keep your mouth shut.

PETS AND PESTS

massacre 'em mozzies

I BOILED some mosquitoes the other day. Not for soup but to kill them. In this land where the Aedes and Culex mosquitoes are the harbingers of the deadly Denggi and Japanese Encephalitis, one has to use whatever means necessary to combat them.

How did I get the mosquitoes into the pot? After steaming rice in a double boiler, I removed the top pot and left the bottom pot uncovered on the stove overnight. The next morning a swarm of mosquitoes have made their way into the pot. I slammed on the lid and turned on the gas. Call me a sadist if you like but the sight of dead mosquitoes floating in their watery grave gave me immense satisfaction.

Recently I accidentally discovered another method of killing mosquitoes. I had done some baking and left the oven door open to cool it down. I forgot to shut the oven door till the next morning. By then an army of mosquitoes had been enticed into its dark interior. I closed the door and turned on the heat till they dropped dead.

Granted these methods of killing mosquitoes are rather unorthodox and are only confined to the kitchen area. A more convenient way of killing them is to wield the insect-zapper like Xena the warrior princess brandishing her sword. It's a battery-operated gadget shaped like a small squash racket. Horizontal wires running across its width carry electric currents which are activated when you press a little knob on the handle.

Walk into a dark corner stealthily. You don't want to alert the enemies with a sudden movement.

Pretend you're Xena and swing your weapon around with vengeance. You'll be rewarded with a fireworks display only to be rivalled by National Day celebration. *Pick-piack! Pick-piack!* The zapper ignites with sparks where the mosquitoes come into contact with the live wires.

Sometimes the zapper only stuns the mosquitoes. To be very certain they go to mosquito heaven, you have to squash them manually. On another surface please, not on the wires. Even after you let go of the knob, the residue current is strong enough to give make your hair stand on end.

If you don't fancy dirtying your hands, press the knob until the mosquitoes go up in flames. The smell of burning mosquitoes is more aromatic than a barbecued chicken drumstick.

If boiling, grilling and electrocuting mosquitoes are not quite your cup of tea, you could always resort to using your bare hands. But this type of mosquito execution needs precision skills. You gotta have a keen eye and a good aim.

Sometimes Lady Luck plays a role. When you're on a roll, you could easily strike nine out of 10. At other times, you're lucky if you hit one out of 10. The downside to all that clapping around is that you end up with sore palms.

Allow me to recommend my husband's techniques. He uses only one hand. The first one is what I call the badminton-smash. He'd follow the flight of the buzzing mosquito, hands raised like a shuttler waiting for his opponent to serve the shuttlecock. When it's within reach, wham! He smashes down on the mosquito as if it's a shuttlecock to be killed in flight. Usually the mosquito is stunned but not dead, yet. He picks it up and proceeds to tear it apart, limb by limb. Does sadism run in the family or what?

The second method is more comical than effective. Imagine a scene in a *kung fu* movie where the hero sits at the table eating his food. A fly buzzes around noisily. The hero shoots out one hand and grabs the fly with his fist. The fly is kaput. In my husband's case, occasionally he gets the mosquito but invariably it flies off when he slowly unclenches his fist.

Of course, there's the very common mosquito killer found on supermarket shelves—the insecticide spray. I remember a television advertisement that was shown many years ago. It showed a woman liberally spraying insecticide all over the dining room while dinner waited at the table. Then without even washing her hands, she sat down at the dining table with her family, all the while extolling the safety of the insecticide.

Oh yeah? Then how come the label on the can says, "Keep away from foodstuff and children." This is off-track but I gotta say this, some advertisers think we've got the brain of mosquitoes.

If you prefer something more environmental-friendly, use my mother-in-law's technique. Smear a plate with cooking oil and wave it around. Mosquitoes which fly into the plate will get stuck on the oil. It works, no kidding.

Or you could let nature take care of its own and leave the mosquitoes to their predator the lizard. Of course, it's not like you could put the lizard on a leash and tell it to "Go get them, boy. Attaboy, lizard! Attaboy!"

them crows are murder

I FOUND a belly-up crow in my garden one morning. Without thinking, I grabbed a broom and dustpan to sweep up the carcass. During this unpleasant but necessary chore, the crows perched on overhead tree branches cawed noisily.

Visions of a motorcyclist being pecked and trailed by dozens of crows suddenly flashed through my mind. It was a picture that appeared in a newspaper sometime ago. Apparently the man did something to one of the crows which caused the flock to relentlessly pursue him every day.

I felt goose pimples popping up my arms. I quickly dumped the dead crow into the dustbin and made a beeline indoors.

The next day I had to wash my extremely dirty car. I parked it in the open driveway and proceeded to apply car shampoo with a rag.

A flock of crows came to rest on the tree branches and electric cables in front of my house. One crow swooped down near my car. I dropped the rag and ran helterskelter into the porch where the birds could not see me.

With heart palpitating wildly like the fluttering wings of a caged-in bird, I waited under the porch for a while. I couldn't let the shampoo dry on the car, so I ventured out again.

Another crow swooped down, then flew up to perch on the television aerial. It watched me warily. With my eyes darting from the aerial to the branches to the cables, I hurriedly washed my car, eager to make my getaway.

I was quite certain then. Yep, those crows were out to get me. What could I do? I didn't fancy being a prisoner in my own house. A brainwave hit me: log onto the Internet to find help.

I surfed to a website which looked pretty authoritative. It was run by the American Society of Crows and Ravens (ASCAR).

They had a list of frequently asked questions (FAQ) and right on top of the list was this question and answer.

"What is a group of crows called, and why? Answer: A 'murder' of crows; this is based on the persistent but fallacious folk tale that crows form tribunals to judge and punish the bad behaviour of a member of the flock.

If the verdict goes against the defendant, that bird is murdered by the flock. The basis in fact is probably that occasionally crows will kill a dying crow which doesn't belong in their territory or much more commonly feed on carcasses of dead crows."

Aaahh ... the mystery of the dead crow in my garden was solved. It was probably an out-of-towner which ended up hurt after a fight, and was then killed by the local crows and dumped in my garden. The murder of crows was probably angry with me for removing their source of food.

Also on the FAQ was a question posed by a surfer from England who wanted to know how he could get rid of a crow which constantly knocked on his window every morning.

The society's answer was, "ASCAR is in the business of admiring corvids, so does not give out information on how to drive them off. But as general advice, learn to enjoy these birds if you are fortunate to have them nearby (e.g. pecking on your window)."

I sympathised with the English bloke. There he was with this problem of a crow with an identity crisis. The bird thought it was a woodpecker and kept pecking at the window ... and ASCAR advised him to enjoy the bird's peck-pecking noise.

These people obviously don't know what it's like to live in a place where crows abound in such numbers that when they take to the skies in a flock, you have to carry an umbrella to ward off bird droppings. Equally annoying is the ruckus they make which is so loud you wish you were wearing earplugs.

Another website said that crows, ravens and magpies are brainy birds as they have the largest overall brain size among their feathered friends. I e-mailed the site founder, Troy, about my predicament.

He responded by e-mailing me another revenge story.

It was written by an American girl who picked up a wounded crow on her way to work. From then on, she was trailed by this murder of crows on her way to work every day.

She was perplexed as to how the crows recognised her when she wore different clothes every time. I am just as baffled and am no closer to the answer either.

Anyway, Troy suggested that I offer the crows food. Er ... excuse me Troy, I appreciate your advice but I want to get rid of 'em crows, not turn my garden into a crow aviary.

As the Internet didn't offer any help whatsoever, I had to think of my own solutions. There were a few options.

I could call the town council and ask them to shoot these winged menaces. If they refuse to come, I may have to move out. I can just imagine the headlines if the newspapers get wind of this. "Woman forced to move house by murder of crows."

Or I could get a catapult and some large stones as arsenal. If the crows try to do something funny like swooping down on me, I'll let fly with a stone and hope it's on target, like how David slayed Goliath the giant.

Or I could blow up some balloons to bursting point. When their cackling becomes unbearable, I'll burst the balloons right under their noses so they'll think the town council guys are after them with their guns.

Scheming for revenge was one thing; putting them into action was a different ball game. My heart is not strong enough to put wings on my plans, so I opted to stay indoors. I think it was an out-of-sight, out-of-mind case for the crows. Luckily, they left me alone.

A few weeks later, I found another crow in my garden.

It was alive but appeared to be hurt. It hopped around the garden until it finally settled on the base of the swing. I wasn't about to remove it for fear that his relatives may think that I was doing it grave bodily harm.

"Could you please come and remove this injured crow out of the garden?" I asked my husband. I didn't add, "And if the crows decide to take revenge, they can go after you. But it's okay, you're out at work most of the time, so you're safe."

Hubby dearest must have seen through my ploy and thought to himself, "I'm home during weekends. Those crows may come after me when all I want to do is to sit out on the swing and enjoy the evening breeze."

He conveniently ignored me. And I ignored the crow.

We went out later and when we returned, the crow was gone. I don't know how. Maybe his brainy relatives came and rescued him. Maybe he slowly hopped out of the garden.

I don't care. As long as I didn't lay a finger on him, his family will leave me alone. And that's all I care about.

# of doggie poo
and doggie pee

WHAT do First Ladies talk about
when they get together? Dog poo. At least that was what I
read in a newspaper article sometime back. I was surprised
that such distinguished ladies would talk about so
mundane a subject. It is a subject that I too can discuss
animatedly with my peers. Not only of dog poo, but of
dog pee, dog flea and dog feed too.

Mostly I talk about the behaviour of our canine and
how my nine-year-old son has to assume full
responsibility for our dog, Einstein. In case, you think this
dog has the brainy ability of his namesake, let me clarify
that this mongrel was given to us by a Chinese-German
friend, hence the German name.

My son Tze Wei loves Einstein. His dad loves dogs
too but he is too busy with work to be involved with the
nitty-gritty of dog rearing, or so he says. So this mummy
who is not too fond of canines (been chased down four
flights of stairs by such a species) spelt out the rules. One,
he has to clean up the dog poo. Two, he is responsible for
bathing him regularly. Three, he must feed the dog.

We do not let Einstein out of the house as we have a
fair-sized compound for him to roam in. He does all his
toileting in the garden. Every morning Tze Wei would
assume his role as the Indah Water sewage tanker. Armed
with an old dustpan and a broken broom stick, he would

keep his eyes peeled to the ground, looking for Einstein's "deposits". When he locates them, he scoops them up and dumps them into a hole specially dug out for this purpose. When the hole is filled up to the brim, dad covers it up with soil and digs another hole.

If Tze Wei shirks his duty for a few days, I would have a hard time when hanging out the laundry in the backyard. My nose can smell the pong from the poo even before my eyes can spot them.

When visitors come acalling, they are greeted by a "Beware of Dog" sign on the gate *and* the putrid stench of dog urine. You see, Einstein likes to pee at the gate and the car tyres.

And I have lost count of the number of flower pots Einstein has broken. Big or small, he has a penchant for darting in between the pots and knocking them down.

If you were to open my refrigerator door, the first thing you would see is a big round aluminium pot. It contains Einstein's chow. Pedigree dog food is too high-class and expensive for our non-pedigree dog. His diet consists of rice with pig's tongue or pig's liver, chicken skin and innards. I cook about a week's supply and dump the whole pot into the fridge. Leftover food, especially chicken and pork bones, go into the pot too.

As a special treat, we would *ta pau* (pack) back a couple of big bones from *bah-kut-teh* (herbal pork stew) for Einstein. He would spend the entire night gnawing at the bones.

Einstein is supposed to get his bath once a week, a routine both canine and master hate, Einstein because he hates to get wet and Tze Wei because of his lazy bones. Due to the irregularity of his baths, Einstein's bony body has become a haven for fleas. These little creatures are well nigh impossible to kill when they are as tiny as ants. You could whack 'em and thump 'em, but after the initial stun, they would continue crawling on their merry way. You have to press down on them with something hard, like a ruler or your finger nails. Fully grown fleas are slightly bigger than beetles and are muddy green in colour. I get immense satisfaction from squishing them with slippers and seeing the blood splotched out on the floor.

Our garden is Einstein's Alcatraz. The chain link fence which separates our neighbours from us are riddled with holes at the bottom, courtesy of Einstein. To prevent him from escaping to the neighbour's, we had to put up chicken coop wiring at the bottom and let the lallang grow to cover up the cracks underneath the fence. On top of that we barricaded it with big slabs of cement blocks.

Unfortunately, or fortunately, depending on whose side you are on, human error allows Einstein to escape from his Alcatraz now and then. When we opened the gate while he wasn't chained, he would race through the open gate with a wild look of abandonment on his face. We would then give chase, sometimes on foot, sometimes on wheels. Even if we managed to track him down, he was not about to relinquish his newfound freedom that easily. When he had his fill of roaming and impregnating strays, he would return on his own accord. After all, he knows where home is.

einstein and his compatriots

AT THE HEIGHT of our dog-owning spree, we had three dogs and two puppies.

We started off with one dog. Einstein, whom we "inherited" from a friend who went to Germany for studies. At that time, my eldest son Tze Wei was seven years old. He wanted a dog badly. So we agreed to let him rear the dog on condition that he fed and bathed him, which he dutifully did. He even acted as poop-scooper as we were living in a house with a small garden and if the poop was not scooped and buried properly, the stink would waft into the house.

Later, another friend gave us a puppy which we named Eddison. This time, the responsibility of feeding the dog fell on Yen Nee. Though Eddison was very mischievous with his feat of chewing shoes and strewing them all over the garden, there were moments when his mischief would crack us up. Like the time when my husband was squatting and doing some gardening with Eddison yapping at his behind. When he stood up, he found Eddison hanging onto his trouser leg like Gnasher was wont to do in the Dennis the Menace comics.

Eddison liked to yap at our feet, especially Tze Ren's who was then a mere toddler. It was funny to see the boy running away from Eddison like someone was firing shots at his feet exclaiming, "Ow! Ow! Ow!" as he fled from the bundle of terror. That was until he discovered that Eddison's tail could be pulled. Then the role was reversed with the little tyke chasing after Eddison.

One day the naughty puppy ran out the gate when it was left open. He only returned a few days later. Not long after that, he ran away again when we inadvertently left the gate open. This time he never came back. He could have been run over by a car for all we know.

Our next dog was Newton which my uncle gave to us. He was a small dog with plenty of fire in him. He and Einstein were at loggerheads, yapping and fighting until both of them were injured. In the end we had to return Newton to my uncle.

Later my brother's friend gave us a female puppy which we named Marie. In the beginning, we let Marie and Einstein roam freely in the garden at night. That wasn't a problem until Marie came "on heat". Einstein kept pouncing on her and she kept refusing his advances. Feeling pity for the little puppy, I let her into the wet kitchen at night. In the daytime, we chained them apart but within sight of each other. For Einstein, it was a case of so close, yet so far. He went completely ballistic, straining on his leash and scratching my car in frustration.

We weighed our options: get her spayed or let her go. We decided on the latter as the previous owner had said that should we decide not to keep her, we could return her. My brother and his friend came and took Marie away. Einstein watched as they put Marie into a box and loaded her into the car. When the car drove off, Einstein started wailing mournfully. He cried for days before he finally got over her. The children, on the other hand, did not miss Marie at all.

Einstein, Eddison, Newton, Marie. Of the lot, only Einstein remains. Tze Wei started to complain that Yen Nee didn't have any dog to feed and that she should share out his workload. So they split the responsibility. Whoever was not doing dishes for the day has to feed the dog.

Our one-dog state lasted for almost two years until someone offered my husband a pair of Boxers, free-of-charge. He was just toying with the idea of breeding dogs for a side-income when the offer came. The opportunity was too good to pass up, he said.

But what about Einstein, I asked. The dogs will go for each other's throats, so it's a toss-up between Einstein and the Boxers unless we can keep them apart.

Tze Wei heard his father saying that we may have to give Einstein away. He moped around for weeks when we were still undecided on the next course of action. One night I found the 12-year-old sniffing away.

"What's wrong?" I asked.

He kept crying.

"Is someone bullying you in school?"

Shake of the head.

"Is your teacher giving you too much homework?"

Another shake.

"Are you sick?"

More sniffles.

Finally he blurted out, "Are we giving Einstein away?"

So, that was what it was all about. Though he may gripe about feeding the dog, he's attached to him. When we first had Einstein and he ran away for days, he cried.

I told hubby that we have to keep Einstein. So, we fenced our garden into two. Einstein stays in the front portion while the newcomers go to the back.

The female Boxer has just given birth to two puppies. We may keep one and sell the other. For now, the kids are marvelling at the puppies. Five-year-old Tze Ren has even named one of them Silin and kept asking me to name the other. I refused to as I didn't want him to get attached to them in case we decide to part company with both. If we do keep one, we may get him to take care of it. It's about time he joined the dog-feeding brigade.

pet sematary

WHEN Tze Wei was nine, he came crying into the kitchen while I was preparing dinner one day. At nine, tears do not come easily to him so I figured it must be something quite upsetting.

His pet fish had died.

After a hug and some words of consolation, he stopped crying and I carried on with my cooking. Later, when I was free to talk to him, I suggested that he bury the fish in the garden. It turned out that he had already done so. He even marked the grave with a brick and two sticks of *lidi* (broom made from the thin stems of coconut fronds) stuck into the ground.

There were other similar incidents. Once, we discovered a bird's nest on our palm tree. We were very excited with the find and brought the nest down from the tree to show the children. We put the nest back where it belonged. We saw the mama bird coming and going from the nest. Then one day, the baby bird died. We found it on the ground. That was the first time Tze Wei had to deal with the sadness of losing an animal friend.

On another occasion, a sickly and scrawny stray kitten wandered into our backyard. We took pity on it and let it stay in the wet kitchen. The next morning we found the kitten had died.

Tze Wei was heart broken even though he barely knew the kitten. To console him, I dug a hole under a palm tree in the garden and buried the kitten there. We even fashioned a cross out of an old hanger to mark the grave. Tze Wei went another step further by writing out an epitaph for the "tombstone". On a page from an old exercise book these words were written neatly: "To my beloved kitten. Goodbye my friend." He hung the paper on the cross. I took it in and covered it with yellow self-adhesive plastic in order to protect it from the elements.

A few months after that incident, a stray puppy found its way into our compound. His mother had abandoned him. He was probably sick, cold and hungry. We put him on a rug and gave him some milk to drink. The puppy whined throughout the whole night. In the morning, we saw that the milk was untouched and the poor puppy had died. Another grave was dug in the garden.

Since then, we have moved to a house with a bigger garden. Like its predecessor, the garden has become a burial ground for animals. This time round, instead of Tze Wei, it was I who experienced the heartache of loss.

Our pair of Boxers, Anak and Laki, had produced two puppies. Initially, we let Anak nurse her litter in the wet kitchen. Two weeks later, we sent them back into the kennel after Anak wolfed down a plate of sausages I was preparing for dinner.

In the evenings, we usually let the dogs out to roam in the garden. One rainy night, we decided not to in order to keep them dry. It was a mistake. The next morning I found the puppies dead. Anak must have trampled them to death while raring to be let out.

I opened the kennel door. Anak picked up one puppy with her mouth and gently deposited it on the cement curb. Then she went back for the other. She whined as she licked her lifeless puppies. Her milk dripped onto the floor. I cried for Anak's loss.

The children were in school and hubby was at work, so I had to dig the grave myself. I shut Anak in before burying the puppies at the other end of the garden.

Not long after that, Laki got injured. Till now, we don't know how the cut was inflicted. Unfortunately we didn't discover the wound until it was too late. By then, it had festered badly. The once-ferocious dog was reduced to a mere whimper of his former self. It was more humane to put him down.

I called in the vet. He took out a syringe from his rectangular medical box and inserted it into the inert dog. Instantaneously, Laki closed his eyes. The vet said something to me but I couldn't answer him for the tears that were choking me up. Poor Laki. If only we had been more vigilant, but at this time "if onlys" are as good as spilt milk.

The vet's assistant put Laki in two layers of light-blue garbage bag and removed the carcass for disposal elsewhere. He was too big to be buried in the garden.

After they left, I cleaned the floor with soap and disinfectant to remove the germs and smell. If only the lumps in my heart could be washed off just as easily.

bye-bye hornets,
wasps and bees

BEES build hives. Hornets and wasps
make paper nests on trees or mud nests on rafters. Fine. As
long as they don't roost on my home ground and
endanger my family. But these insects are no respecter of
property. Like squatters, they build anywhere they like.
And they happen to like my house and garden very much.

Two years ago, my husband discovered what we
thought was a bee hive hanging about three metres up our
mango tree. It was pear-shaped and the size of a
basketball. We called in the firemen. They came to check
it out and pronounced that it was a hornet's nest, not a bee
hive. We set a date for the extermination. The firemen
asked us to prepare some kerosene, rags, wire and a
gunnysack for the job.

The firemen briefed us on the modus operandi. The
nest has to be burned at night so that the hornets can't see
where to fly. According to an Internet check, this is the
best time to destroy the nest as the hornets would be
resting and not out foraging for food somewhere.

On the appointed date, a group of five firemen
trooped to my house. They tied the rags to a long pole
with the wire, doused it with kerosene and lighted it up.
We switched off all the lights in the house as instructed
and went upstairs to watch. We had a good view from my
son's room. The ball of fire touched the nest and it caught

fire immediately, licking up the surrounding leaves with a crackling sound.

It was over in five minutes. The nest fell to the ground. When the fire had died down, they nudged the burnt-out nest into the gunnysack and secured it at the neck. If any hornet had survived the inferno, it wouldn't have been able to bite its way through the sack.

These critters are omnipresent. Though we've just exterminated one nest, more hornets came. Their next stop was in my wet kitchen cum laundry area where they could freely fly in and out of the grilled enclosure. Some hornets or perhaps they're wasps (according to my trusty encyclopaedia, hornets are a type of large wasps) made a nest on one of the wooden rafters right above my stove. From a blob of mud, it kept getting bigger till it became the size of my palm. When the pest controller came on a follow-up visit for a termite-control package we had taken earlier, I asked them to remove the nest. They scraped off the caked mud from the beam and sprayed it with a smelly chemical.

Bees have joined in the fray too. The wooden beams supporting the grilles became a target for carpenter bees. They bored holes the size of a 20-sen coin in the wood to nest. I have to run for cover when the bees hovered too close for comfort. They would buzz around the beams looking for their nest and upon finding it, they'd "zoop" inside. I complained about the bees to my brother who happened to be there doing some repair work on the gutter. He promptly sealed up the holes with filler with a bee just "zooped" in still inside.

When the rest of the gang came looking for their nest, they couldn't find the hole. So they bored another hole and continued to buzz around while I cook or hang up the laundry. Then one day, they stopped coming to the nest. Perhaps they had tunnelled to where their friend was entombed and decided to shift to a safer place.

Sometime last year, the grasscutter discovered another hornet's nest on a Christmas tree. It was suspended about one metre off the ground. The unkempt bougainvillea and Japanese canna had hidden it from view. The nest was about the size of a football. When I told my husband about calling in the firemen again, he said, "No need, we can do it ourselves." So I waited for him to "do it ourselves." Month after month went by without any action.

Then one day the newspaper frontpaged the news of a 10-year-old girl who was purportedly stung to death by a bee. That sent me flying to the fire department. This time, they didn't bother to make an assessment trip. They came that very night after asking us to prepare the required paraphernalia. By now, the nest had ballooned to the size of a car tyre!

The three firemen shook their heads when they saw the small mineral-bottle of kerosene I had provided.

"Not enough kerosene," they said. "The nest is too big. We need petrol for more power. Otherwise we may end up in the hospital with hornet-stings."

Using a hose, they tried to siphon off some petrol from my car. They couldn't. So I hopped to the nearest petrol station to buy some petrol. I brought along an empty 1.5 litre soft-drink bottle to contain the fuel. The attendant put the nozzle into the bottle and pumped two ringgit's worth of petrol into the bottle. It looked like urine.

Back home, the three firemen had tied up all five pieces of rag and the gunnysack around a metal tube about three centimetres in diameter. They took the bottle of petrol with nods of approval. As before, we switched off the lights and went upstairs to watch. The fireman who was supposed to hold the tube had donned a thick protective suit consisting of overall, gloves and head cover, looking like a bee-keeper.

In no time, the nest was licked by large tongues of flame. Less than five minutes later, the tube holder ran outside the house and plunged the ball of fire into the drain. Mission accomplished. Now I could breathe easy.

It may sound cruel, this fiery extermination of hornets. After all, they play a necessary role in nature. Hornets and wasps feed on smaller insects such as flies while bees pollinate flowers. But when they come too close for comfort, I say let the flies and flowers be, it's bye-bye to the hornets, wasps and bees.

IN THE FAMILY WAY

and baby makes six

SEPTEMBER 2000. We were having dinner at home. Hubby and I had an important piece of news for our children, Tze Wei, Yen Nee and Tze Ren aged ten, nine and three respectively.

"We're going to have another baby," I announced.

Silence. Tze Wei's forehead wrinkled up in a frown.

"Why must you have another baby? He may be naughty like Tze Ren," he muttered.

"Yeah. He always messes up my room," Yen Nee chipped in.

The children's faces were as long as papayas. The only one showing some enthusiasm was Tze Ren. He wanted to know where the baby was and peered into my sleeve to look for the baby. When told that the baby was inside mummy's tummy, he lifted up my shirt to look for it.

Due to my morning sickness, I couldn't stomach any strong smells so I stopped cooking altogether for two months. The prospect of having another sibling to contend with was already unattractive to the older children. To add salt to the injury, they had to put up with catered food, which was not to their liking. On top of that, Tze Wei had to cook rice everyday as lethargy got the better of me.

They had to take turns with their father to massage my aching shoulders. Tze Wei has strong hands that can give an invigorating massage, so he did the lion's share of the work. He moaned and groaned until his father promised him a reward for his massaging services. He would get an extra allowance to buy any books he wanted after the baby was born.

Though I had shown the baby's ultrasound picture to the children, they didn't quite know what to make of the black and white blurred image. But as they saw the baby's paraphernalia accumulating, their anticipation grew. We took back the baby cot that we had lent my sister. My brother had a stroller that his sons had outgrown, so we borrowed it as ours was about to fall apart (three babies had used it in the span of seven years). We borrowed the steriliser from my sister-in-law and bought baby bottles and pacifiers. We collected the secondhand baby clothes from my mother, who stored them after each grandchild had outgrown them.

As this was our fourth child, my husband and I were quite lax on the preparation. I remember, when we were expecting Tze Wei, we had put up the baby cot and packed my hospital bag two months in advance. With this one, the children had to keep asking us, "When are you going to put up the baby cot" before my husband eventually set it up, two days before the baby's due date.

Seeing the baby cot decorated with ribbons and soft toys with the little pillow and bolster laid out on it, the children became more excited. Was it going to be a girl or a boy? We didn't know. What's the baby's name going to be? We were still undecided over the names suggested by my in-laws.

In keeping with her siblings' tradition of arriving late into the world, Khoo Su Yen finally made her appearance six days after the due date. That night when her brothers and sister came to visit at the hospital, they looked in fascination at the tiny pink baby swaddled in a pink blanket. She's got them wrapped around her little fingers.

When I returned home from the hospital, Tze Ren still wanted to kiss my tummy like he used to. He thought the baby was still in there. He didn't understand that the baby had been born and that she is little Su Yen.

All three children were gentle with the baby. Most of the time she would lie in the big, rectangular bouncinet which took pride of place in the centre of the living room. They learned to rock her. When she became sturdier and lost some of the babyish floppiness, Tze Wei and Yen Nee learnt how to carry her. Tze Wei was more confident while Yen Nee, who was smaller in build, was less assured but she gradually became more adept at holding her. Even Tze Ren who is five years old now can carry her by hooking his hands under her arms.

As Su Yen grows, so does her siblings' affection towards her. We call her the cutest baby in the whole universe. My husband "tsked tsked" at this gross exaggeration, but to us, that is what she is, our cutest, sweetest baby.

The older children like to watch Su Yen's cute antics. They laugh at her funny expressions when she tries out new food. They beamed with pride when they witnessed her taking her first steps. When they see her crying pitifully in the playpen, they take her out even though they may be in the thick of homework. They smother her with kisses.

Without a doubt, Su Yen has wriggled into their hearts and transformed the initial animosity into warmth and affection.

morning sickness blues

SOME WOMEN are so blessed. They breeze through their pregnancy with nary a puke nor puff. Alas! I'm not one of them. I had to retch and gag through the first trimester of every pregnancy. Now entering the third trimester of my fourth pregnancy, I can afford to write about the unpalatable experience without throwing up.

The term "morning sickness" is deceiving as it doesn't just happen in the morning. It can strike any time of the day. For me, it was particularly bad in the evenings. When dinner time came, I could hardly eat a morsel. I would crawl into bed as early as eight o'clock to quell the nausea and ignore my growling stomach. Sometime in the morning, any time between one and six o'clock, my tummy would wake me up. Then only would I have my "dinner" of Milo and biscuits.

It's strange that through out all four pregnancies, I acquired an aversion to rice. No matter how fluffy the rice was or how delicious the accompanying dishes were, they had become as appetising as uncooked grains. My diet consisted mainly of noodles, biscuits and bread. It didn't really matter what I ate anyway because most of it would end up in the toilet bowl.

The consumption of liquids was another dicey matter. Plain water has never tasted so bland and plain. I drank plenty of sugar-cane juice and coconut water. When the hawker near my house didn't show up, I had to resist the urge to drive a few kilometres just to buy from the next hawker.

You know the weird taste you get in your mouth when you're ill? When everything tastes flat and unappetising, including your own saliva? That's exactly how it was for me all the time.

I had to pop sweets into my mouth throughout the day and night. Not just any sweet, mind you, it has to be the sour plum flavour. Other sweets were either too sweet, too hot, too something or other. I always stashed a pouch of those sweets in my handbag. Only one sundry shop near my house sells that particular variety and I cleaned them out of their stock of sour plum sweets. During this pregnancy alone, I consumed more than 150 sweets.

Morning sickness not only played havoc with my tastebuds but also my nostrils. Every smell is magnified many times over. Whether it's the smell of slaughtered chicken in the market, herbs in the *sinseh*'s (Chinese medicine practitioner) shop or freshly-cut grass in the garden, they made my life miserable.

For this reason, I stopped going to the market. I stopped cooking as the smell of frying onions or *ikan bilis* stock made me nauseous.

But I couldn't stop my neighbours from cooking. Both my immediate neighbours are housewives and they cook twice a day. I used to relish the aroma of their cooking—chicken *kurma*, *rendang*, fish curry and other tantalising food—but not during my pregnancy. A slight whiff of their cooking would have me bolting all my doors and windows to prevent the odours from wafting into my house.

My ultra-sensitive nose also prevented me from going to the supermarket. The hodgepodge of odours that prevailed within its air-conditioned interiors is too much for me to bear. The aroma of ripening fruits and waffles toasting in the waffle-making machine mingling with the smell of fish and chicken was akin to the stale smell of a food-laden, switched-off fridge. In one word: yucky!

An incident that happened in my second month of pregnancy made me avoid the supermarkets as though they were stocked up with barrels of rotting fish. My family and I had eaten lunch at the food court of a shopping complex before adjourning to the supermarket section.

I felt queasy after the meal. So while the rest of the family shopped, I rested on one of those black massage chairs, trying to suppress the queasiness. When the shopping was done, we decided to go home as I was still feeling nauseous. Everything was under control until we got out of the lift to go home. The jerking of the lift had triggered off my vomiting button. I quickly pulled out my emergency plastic bag and let go into it. Fried noodles and Sprite came pouring out as if a tap had been turned on full blast. My kids who cannot stand the sight of people vomiting, ran helter-skelter to the car while passersby stared.

I tried not to go out unnecessarily. Still I had to ferry the children to school and run errands. My children know what to expect when I veer off to the road shoulder or when I open the door at the red lights.

Wherever possible, I confined myself to the house, as lethargic as a zombie and as weak as an invalid. Morning sickness had been the bane of all my pregnancies. Unfortunately, one does not become more adept at handling the malady, no matter how many times one goes through it.

First pregnancy or fourth, the taste of bile in the mouth when every morsel of food had been thrown up was just as bitter. The sight and aroma of food was just as disgusting.

Having said that, I'm glad that my morning sickness only lasted two to three months. I know of some people who had to endure it for the entire nine months. Yet others were afflicted so badly they had to be put on drips. Compared to these hapless women, my pregnancy was a breeze.

a letter to my unborn baby

MY DEAREST BABY in the womb,
You are now 30 weeks old. In another eight weeks or so, you would be ready to make your entrance into this world. I hope you would not delay your coming for too long. Your two brothers and sister made mummy wait. I hope you will be punctual.

If you're early by a few days, that's even better. At least I get to save a few days of carrying my big belly with you sloshing around in it. As it is, at 30 weeks, my belly looks extraordinarily big, as if you're a full-term baby. But the doctor's calculation shows that you're average in size. I certainly hope you will not get too big, so that you'll have an easier passage into the world and mummy won't need to have an operation to get you out.

People are always asking, "Have you had your scan already or not? Is it a boy or a girl?" And I reply, "Yes, I've had a scan but I chose not to know your sex." Then they say, "Yeah, after all, you already have both a boy and a girl."

It would be a bonus if you are a girl, to provide girly company for your sister. But if you are a boy, that's fine too. Your sister would get to be the "princess" of the family. What mummy prays for constantly is that you be born healthy, with no defects or disabilities. At my age, the odds of you being a Down's Syndrome baby is one in 200. I pray that you'd be among the 199.

The doctor had asked if I wanted an amniocentesis done. This is the test where doctors draw out some amniotic fluid from the womb to test if you have Down's Syndrome. My answer was a firm "no" because even if I knew for certain that you're going to be a Down's baby, I would not do anything to hurt you. I would still keep you and love you. So, what's the point of the amniocentesis? It would be a waste of money and may result in more anxiety.

Everyday I can feel you moving inside me. A flutter here and a kick there assure mummy you're progressing fine. I just can't wait for you to be born. I wonder whom you would look like. Will you look like daddy or mummy?

Your siblings do not resemble each other. Your eldest brother looks like daddy with a typical Chinese face. Your sister looks a little like mummy—both of us are constantly mistaken as Malays. Your second brother looks like he has a Caucasian for a parent. Friends jokingly asked if we had brought back the wrong baby from the hospital. Of course, we hadn't!

Perhaps the fact that mummy's late grandpa was adopted had something to do with it. For all we know, your great-grandfather could be descended from an *ang moh*. In fact, his nickname was *ang moh*, a Hokkien word meaning "red hair" which is a colloquial term for Caucasian.

Speaking of your second brother, I wonder if you're going to recognise his voice after you're born. He is the one who has been rubbing mummy's tummy frequently and saying, "I want to kiss baby," and then giving mummy's tummy a peck. When you were very small and hadn't made mummy's tummy balloon up yet, he used to look for you in my sleeve or under my shirt. Now he knows where you are. He is going to be four years old in May, the same month that you are due. He can be very mischievous but is also very affectionate.

Your eldest brother and sister will help mummy to take care of you after you're born. At first they were not very excited when they heard that you were coming into the family. But they are getting used to the idea. They just hope that you will not be as naughty as your second brother.

And, of course, your daddy will love you too. You are our "surprise package," one whom we will cherish. He is good with babies. In fact, he helped to take care of your siblings when they were babies too, so you can rest assured that you'll be in good hands.

See you soon. Not too soon, but not too late either, okay?

Love,
Mummy

house arrest

IMAGINE this scenario: You cannot bathe or wash your hair for an entire month. Forget about shopping, visiting friends or even going for a stroll in the neighbourhood. Ginger, sesame oil and Chinese wine will dominate your diet and you can't drink water as you please.

Sounds like a new form of house arrest? In a way, it is. Welcome to the confinement period mandatory for Chinese mothers, so termed for obvious reasons.

The purpose of the month-long confinement period, a centuries-old tradition, is to nurture the mother's health back to its pre-natal state. The emphasis is on keeping the body warm and driving out *fong* (wind) which has entered the mother's body during childbirth. A general practitioner would call *fong* flatulence, but a *sinseh* (practitioner of traditional Chinese medicine) would call it the element which produces pain that is not localised. It's like the natural phenomenon of wind which blows, stops or changes direction. *Fong* that is not eliminated after pregnancy is believed to bring on an onslaught of ailments such as rheumatism, headaches and backaches during old age.

Crucial to the confinement is the *pui yuet*, Cantonese for 'companion for a month'. The *pui yuet*'s job is to cook and care for the mother, baby and other children throughout the confinement period. Those who can afford it hire a *pui yuet*. But sometimes a mother or mother-in-law is substituted either out of financial consideration, respect, or inability to procure a *pui yuet* due to high demand.

My mother is a professional and highly-regarded *pui yuet*. She agreed to be my *pui yuet* for my third child, as she had been for my second. A few days before my due date, she purchased the core ingredients for my special diet: a few kilogrammes of old ginger, a few bottles of Chinese red wine, rice wine and Benedictine DOM brandy, sesame oil, packets of red and black dates, and Chinese herbs such as *ghizhi* (medlar seeds), *tong kuei* (angelica) and *tong sum* (codonopsis root). These herbs are believed to improve blood circulation and revitalise health.

The Chinese have two basic classifications of food, cooling and heating. Too much cooling food—such as leafy vegetables and melons—is believed to produce *fong*, muscle cramps and rheumatism. However, excessive heating food—such as beef, spices, brandy, and fruits like durian—causes *yuet hei* (hot air). The symptoms of this ailment are dry throat and lips. The idea is to strike a good balance, and not to eat an excess of either type of foods.

Rice, pork, poultry and certain fish such as white pomfret are said to be neutral, but their qualities can be altered by the method of cooking. Frying food imbues it with the heating element, whereas steaming food is cooling. Old ginger, sesame oil and rice wine reinforce the heating elements of food. That is why the confinement diet uses an excessive amount of these three ingredients.

I still remember vividly the confinement meal I ate after my most recent birth. It had been a difficult delivery. What little food I ate hours before the onslaught of labour had been expended during childbirth. My stomach was growling with hunger. A whiff of the food's aroma made my mouth water. Mum had cooked thin slices of pig kidney, pig liver, lean pork and juliennes of ginger with sesame oil and Chinese wine. Not even a grain of rice remained on my plate when I finished.

That was how it was for every meal. On the fifth day, leftovers became common. I had tired of the same old food: pork and chicken cooked in lots of sesame oil and Chinese wine. To provide variation, mum sometimes deep-fried chicken pieces and pork slices instead. Shredded old ginger, besides being used as a flavouring, can be deep-fried to make a tasty side dish. Thankfully, after a fortnight, the diet included white pomfret which is good for stimulating breast milk, broccoli and french beans.

There is less flexibility in the consumption of liquids. I was only allowed to quench my thirst with red dates tea. Every night mum put some red dates, *tong sum*, dried longan and medlar seeds into a slow cooker. By morning, the fragrant aroma of the tea permeated the kitchen. She kept the tea warm in a thermos flask. Throughout the day I drank the red dates tea instead of plain water. I yearned for plain water. Mum constantly warned me about the consequences of drinking plain water which purportedly makes the veins swell. I tested out the theory in her absence. My veins didn't swell but I refrained from cheating too often lest I get caught. No point in bringing on the lectures from mum and mother-in-law who kept reminding me to comply with the rules.

Every night I drank a special brew of chicken essence, ginger juice and brandy. It was like drinking chili-flavoured syrup which I quickly washed down with red dates tea to mask the strong taste. The soup never failed to bring on streams of sweat.

Considering my scanty personal hygiene practice, perspiration only added to my "unclean" condition. For nine days after delivery, I didn't bathe at all. I dry-cleaned by sponging myself with a towel rinsed in hot boiled water.

On the tenth day, I was allowed my first bath with water boiled with ginger and lemon grass. The brew resembled drain water, not very alluring for a bath. But after nine days of dry cleaning, it was immaterial whether the water was brown, yellow or green. The feel of the water running down my body was ecstasy, though the water was very hot. This is supposed to prevent *fong* from entering the body. Mum repeatedly asked me not to add cold water to it knowing that I might cheat. I did—behind closed doors.

The most unbearable taboo was abstaining from washing my hair. Not even one drop of water must touch the head to keep the highly feared *fong* at bay. The days inched by slowly. Later I grew accustomed to my dirty hair which must have gained a few grams of weight in dust and grime. Dry shampoo— coarse white powder rubbed into the scalp, then brushed off—helped a little in ridding the smell and oiliness. When I finally got to wash my hair albeit with ginger water on the thirtieth day, my head felt as light as a floating balloon. I imagined I was a model in a shampoo advertisement, swinging my hair to show off its bounce.

Rest is important to hasten recuperation. I wasn't allowed to do anything strenuous. Even carrying my baby for too long was considered an overexertion. The days stretched by boringly with nothing to do but sleep, eat and lie around. Sitting up too much is frowned upon as it may produce backaches later on in life. Activities that taxed the eyes too much like watching television and reading are also discouraged. One can grow mouldy with inactivity. Visiting friends and relatives provide the only relief from monotony.

It is also taboo for the mother to leave the house. As the emphasis is on keeping the body warm, the likelihood of catching a chill is greater outdoors. If I were to so much as step out onto the porch, mum would quickly shoo me inside.

So many taboos, so little logic. Though that may be so, many like myself decide to play it safe. One month of discomfort is a small price to pay to avoid ailments which may plague us later in life.

BLESSED ARE
THE CHILDREN

Bigger is better

MY GRANDMOTHERS have nine each. My mother have six. I have four. Children, that is.

Though the downward trend is obvious from my family's genealogy, what isn't so clear is the fact that four offspring by today's standards is considered super-productive. Gone are the days when families the size of a football team flourished like grass on fertile soil. Today, the big families are relay and basketball teams of four and five respectively as opposed to smaller units of doubles and *sepak takraw* squads.

Worried about the Chinese's decreasing fertility rate in Malaysia, one clan association is providing a RM2,000 cash incentive for the fourth baby produced by its members. Whilst it should be given a pat on the back for its initiative, in the big scheme of raising kids, this sum is but a mere speck in the desert. The likelihood of it inducing people to make more babies is as remote as a camel going through the eye of a needle. Our neighbours down south don't know how lucky they are to be offered cash bonuses for six years for only the second and third babies.

Though two grand is a pittance, I wish I belonged to that clan association so that I could get my hands on that money. Half a loaf, or in this case even the crust, is better than nothing at all. At least it could have helped defray the cost of delivery charges at the hospital.

More kids mean more expenses—food, clothing, education policies and a bigger car if you have as many kids as there are car windows. When we were expecting number four, we traded in our jalopy for an MPV. It's nothing fancy, mind you. We could only afford the cheapest model available but it has more than enough seats for our needs. If you tell that to our kids though, they'd disagree. They still jostle for space if one of them decides to stretch out. One of these days we should trade in the MPV for a minibus—then they can have all the seats they want.

Beyond the ringgit sense, there are other factors that come into play when determining the size of the family. One of these is the equation of "more kids = more noise". If you're the peace-loving type, forget about having more kids. You have to hear constant wailings of "Mummy! You see *chieh chieh* won't give me the cushion!" or "Mummy! *Ko ko* tell me to shaddup!" or "Mummy! Su Yen is sticking the spoon up her nose!"

Another word of caution. The hullabaloo children make when playing or quarrelling is like stereo speakers blasting out rock music on max multiplied by the number of kids.

While on this subject, you'd better be prepared to get as many radio sets as there are children. On some days three radios in my house are turned on simultaneously. Downstairs, hubby is listening to Light & Easy. In elder daughter's room, Taiwanese girl band, S.H.E., is playing loudly on the CD player. Eldest son is listening to Blue while doing his homework. Lately he has taken a liking to

Linkin Park whose music sounds like clanging cymbals to my ears. I shudder to think of the time when my preschooler and toddler come of age and want to listen to their own brand of music, too.

Having a big family could also put a damper on your social life. It seems to me like we used to get more meal invitations when we had fewer than four kids. Maybe we've become more reclusive. Whatever it is, big families tend to stay home more, especially when the children are younger, and going out is like moving house, what with lugging along the baby bag, stroller and other paraphernalia.

Does it seem like I'm building up a case against large families? Certainly not, I'm just preparing you for the worst-case scenario. I've reserved the best for last.

Having more offspring is good. It means more children to love, more cherubic faces to kiss and more bottoms to pinch. It means more helping hands to do the dishes, wash the car or massage mummy's aching shoulders. It means more cards on Mother's Day and Father's Day. It means more companionship; when the older children leave the nest, the younger ones are still around to warm the roost. It means more people at family gatherings and more heads in family portraits. Last but not least, it means a longer name list in obituaries.

By all means, go for more.

kids on errands

RUNNING ERRANDS with young children tagging along can be a hassle. Whether it's dashing into the grocery shop to pick up some eggs or the ATM machine to withdraw money, it's easier to leave the kids in the car with the engine running. Despite the niggling worry that something untoward may happen, convenience usually wins the day for me.

Whenever I leave the car, I always lock the door to prevent strangers from jumping in and driving off. My five-year-old son knows the routine—lock the door when mummy gets out and unlock it when she returns. One day I discovered just how well he knows the drill.

I had dropped by my mother's place to pick up something. I left Tze Ren and my one-year-old girl in the car. While talking to my mother, I noticed that he had alighted from the car to retrieve the letters sticking out from the postbox. When we all wanted to get back into the car, we found that we had been locked out and my handbag with the spare key was INSIDE the car.

"Tze Ren, why did you lock the door?" I asked in consternation.

"So bad guys cannot go in."

I wanted to laugh and strangle him at the same time.

I tried to unlock the door using the wire hook of a clothes hanger like I've seen others doing. After fiddling with it for a few minutes without making any progress, I gave up. My neighbour went to get a locksmith who managed to undo the lock. My baby was securely strapped down in her car seat so she was none the worse for the adventure except for crying her eyes out.

That incident adds another rule for Tze Ren. "Never lock the door when Su Yen is inside the car alone." Not when he wants to get down to retrieve the mail, or when he wants to get down to urinate or whenever I stop the car, which could be anywhere—at the supermarket, the clinic, my mother's or anywhere for that matter.

Recently I went to the bank. The minute we alighted from the car, he wanted to *shhee-shhee*. He spotted a hole at the side of the road. He pulled down his trousers discreetly and aimed into the hole. I stood a little distance from him, near enough to protect him but far away to disavow any acquaintance with him should anybody chide me for treating the road like a public toilet.

Later we had lunch at a nearby shopping complex. I was still feeding Su Yen when Tze Ren guzzled up his last morsel of waffle. He stood around people-watching. Then I saw him clutched his fly.

"Mummy, I want to *shhee-shhee* again."

"But you just did it a while ago. You have to hold it for a while, okay?" I said crossly. Why didn't he finish the job just now?

I packed up and paid for the food. The cashier said the nearest toilet was on the second floor. No way we were going to make it there on time from the ground floor. The little fella's legs were already twisting left and right to prevent a leak.

We ran out of the building. He knew what to look for. It's a hole in the road, a drain or plants. There were some pots of bougainvillaea outside. Quickly he pulled down his pants and squirted his special brand of fertiliser on the soil while I try to look unrelated to him with my nonchalance.

At the supermarket later, Tze Ren was at it again. This time he grasped his buttocks. Uh-oh, big business calling.

Pushing the baby in the shopping trolley, we raced to the toilet like we were on a supermarket sweep competition. I couldn't wheel the trolley in as there wasn't a ramp leading up the steps. So I carried Su Yen in.

Tze Ren barged into an empty stall and plopped himself down on the toilet seat. Meanwhile I felt the urge to ease myself too. As I didn't want to leave Su Yen unattended in the trolley outside, I took her into the cubicle with me. Answering nature's call in a narrow cubicle—with a baby in one arm while wearing zippered pants, required some sweat-inducing calisthenics but I did it without any mishap.

When Tze Ren had finished his business, I opened the door to see him leaning comfortably against the toilet cistern.

"Don't lean back! The toilet is dirty!" I screamed.

He smiled sweetly and got up. Teetering a little off balance as his trousers lay at a puddle on his feet, he bent down, touching the wet floor with his hands.

"Don't touch the floor! It's dirty!"

He moved his hands from the floor to my ankles.

With a half-naked boy bent double at my feet, a baby perched on my hips and hands digging frantically for tissues in my handbag, we were a comical sight to behold.

I mustn't shop alone with these two until they're older.

# of bananas and apples

SUSAN and her family migrated to Australia when her firstborn was barely a year old. A few years later when recession hit Australia and they had to return to Malaysia for a stint, they came back with two additional offspring. Not surprisingly, all her children couldn't speak a word of Chinese; in fact, one of them spoke English with a heavy Aussie accent.

Some folks called her kids "bananas"—yellow on the outside, white on the inside. Since their return though, they have picked up some Chinese and learnt Malay.

Though "banana" is hardly a complimentary monicker, it's a rather apt description of a Chinese who can't speak his mother tongue but is fluent in English. "Bananas" are propagating more abundantly than ever in the fertile environment of nuclear families who don't converse in their mother tongue.

I read somewhere that the Native Americans who don't speak their native language are called "apples": red on the outside, white on the inside. Looks like this phenomenon is not confined to the Chinese alone.

Anyway, my children could just as easily have turned out to be "bananas". My husband and I are English-educated. We speak English at home. It is the language that our children was first introduced to. They grow up speaking English and thinking in English. In their young minds, they are English, not Chinese. When they grew older, they understood that speaking English doesn't make them English and that they are Chinese.

All of my siblings except one are Chinese-educated. They speak Mandarin with their children. So does my mother who used to babysit my older kids. Therefore my children's first brush with Mandarin was with their grandmother and cousins. We sent them to a Chinese school so that they'll get a good grounding in the Chinese language; the other reason being, of course, "China is opening up." Now they can read and write fairly well in Chinese though they still prefer to communicate in English.

When it comes to Hokkien which is the dialect of my husband and I, it is a different story altogether. I'm reminded of an incident which my father-in-law likes to relate. One day he was at the shopping complex with my sister-in-law's preschooler. The boy saw something he wanted to buy but grandpa refused to buy it for him. There was a communication breakdown as grandpa couldn't speak English and grandson didn't understand a word of Chinese. A scene ensued when the kid bawled his lungs out. The security guard accused my father-in-law of kidnapping the boy because "if you're his grandpa, why can't he understand you?"

When they were younger, my children's grasp of Hokkien was like my nephew's. With exposure, they have gradually come to understand more of the dialect. Now they can comprehend most of what we say but they find it awkward to converse in Hokkien. And when they do, they sound like Mat Sallehs grappling with a foreign tongue.

I had tried unsuccessfully to institute "Hokkien only" sessions, when on any given evening I might say during dinnertime, "Okay, let's speak Hokkien only for the rest of the night". The kids would giggle as the conversation progressed. By the time dinner was over, after countless interruptions of "what's the meaning of this or that" and "how to say such-and-such in Hokkien," we would have reverted to English.

Strangely enough if my husband and I purposely speak in Hokkien when discussing "adult" matters, they can quickly grasp the gist of our conversation and want to join in too.

It was the same with my friends' children. Not too long ago, a friend and I were having tea with her seven-year-old son in tow. When our conversation turned gossipy, we switched to Hokkien. From the corner of my eyes, I could see the boy sidling up closer and his ears perking up like a doggie standing at attention. Even with his rudimentary understanding of the dialect, he managed to figure out what we were talking about.

On linguistic training, perhaps I should take a leaf from a relative who successfully taught her children to speak English and German. The fact that her husband is a German probably helped but credit should be given for her effective yet simple system. When they are in their rooms, they speak English. Once they're out of their rooms, German's the way to go. And they speak Malay, Mandarin and Hokkien too, though not as fluently.

Some folks have other systems. English-educated daddy would speak English to the kids while Chinese-educated mummy would converse in Mandarin.

I've not been very rigorous in teaching Hokkien to my children. Perhaps it's time to put in more concerted efforts as I do want them to be able to converse comfortably in Hokkien. I think that the ability to communicate in their own dialect is a way for them to stay in touch with their own culture. If they don't learn it, neither would their children and by the time their grandchildren arrive, dialects may have gone the way of the dinosaurs.

toilet training su yen

BABY Su Yen began her toilet-training the day she came back from the hospital. My mum who helped me during the one-month confinement is a firm believer of potty-training from birth.

Every morning before she gave Su Yen her bath, mum puts her on the potty. The newborn babe was propped in a semi-reclining position, with her bottom touching only half of the oversized potty rim. Periodically throughout the day, mum would go through the motion of putting the baby on the potty. Soon Su Yen learnt to urinate and defecate into the potty.

Friends were amazed at this toilet-trained baby who could *shhee-shhee* and *poo-poo* on cue. And I was delighted that nappy-washing and cleaning-up "accidents" were kept to a minimum. On some days, I only had three or four nappies to wash. When the timing was not so accurate, I might end up with a dozen nappies though.

Things changed when Su Yen started to walk. She began to digress in her toilet-training. No matter how long or how hard I say, "ssshhhhhh ..." the urine refused to flow when she sat on the potty. The nappies piled up. What was worse was cleaning up the big mess. Before, I only had to say "nnnggg, nnnggg ..." to bring on the desired result. But at that stage, she didn't seem to understand the word anymore.

From then on, her nappy liners disappeared fast as I disposed the soiled pieces instead of washing them. One box of 100 liners that had lasted her many months, was depleted in two months.

If the mess was contained in her nappy or disposable diapers, cleaning up was relatively easy. But when the poo-poo spill out of her nappy and into everything she came into contact with, that was when I get hopping-mad. I remember one hair-pulling day filled with smelly misadventures when she soiled not only herself, but the pillows, cushions, toys and playpen. I had to wash the baby, pillow covers, cushion covers, toys and playpen. My neighbour must have wondered at the Lego blocks, toy cars, plastic figurines and finger puppet king and queen perched atop my chain link fence.

"Naughty girl! Always give mummy extra work!" was my favourite grouse while I launched into a frenzy of cleaning.

"Why do you scold her? It's not her fault," my husband said.

Yeah, yeah, I know it wasn't her fault and it's had nothing to do with naughtiness. But when you had to wash slimy bottoms and scrub soiled nappies day in and day out, sometimes several times a day, it was difficult to whistle while you work. Besides, he wasn't the one doing the dirty work.

Lately Su Yen made some progress. She would say "*nnnggg-nnnggg*" as she pat her bottom, but the warning came *after* she has passed motion. Then came another improvement. This time she would say "nnnggg-nnnhgg" *before* she did it. Unfortunately, when I put her on the potty, she refused to sit on it for more than a minute. She could go through the motion of sitting down and getting up repeatedly without so much as a drop being expelled. When I'm tired of the charade, I'd put away the potty, which seemed to be her cue for letting go.

At nineteen months, the girl appeared to understand the significance of the word "*nnnggg-nnnggg*", or rather the response it could invoke. When she was fed-up of being cooped up in the play-pen and wanted to be let out, she would say the magical word and she'd be quickly whisked out into freedom. When she had enough of sitting on the high-chair and wants to boycott her food, "*nnnggg- nnnggg*" was her key to liberty.

I know what the books say about toilet-training. Don't be anxious about it, don't apply undue pressure, don't scold the child, let her do it when she's ready and so on. I should know, Su Yen is my fourth child. But good advice and experience count for nothing when garlic was browning in the wok, the phone was ringing incessantly, the newspaper vendor was at the gate to collect her dues, the rain was falling and the laundry was still out on the clothesline AND there came an urgent yell of "Mummy!" from the kids which could only mean that a stinky accident has happened.

I tried to take it easy. If she can go potty at the right time, *yipee yeah yeah*! Otherwise, just clean up the mess quietly and don't take it out on her. Sometimes I couldn't resist giving her a smack on the bottom.

The day did come when she went to the potty without any prompting. There was no looking back from then on. Hurray! My two-year-old has graduated from toilet-training school with flying colours!

money matters

IT IS ESSENTIAL to teach children about the value of money and the importance of work. And the best way to do that is to make them earn their own money. My children used to think that money grow not on trees, but banks. If mummy has no money, she just has to go to the bank to withdraw money. Their perception is not wrong, just incomplete. I explained that first, daddy has to work to earn money for keeping in the bank, otherwise the bank will not give us any money.

Tze Wei and Yen Nee started earning their own money when they were about six years old. We gave them small chores to perform such as washing their own dishes. They were awarded points which would be converted to cash at the end of every month. They used the money to buy treats for themselves such as potato chips, ice-cream or fancy stationery.

When they attended primary school, they got a daily allowance of fifty sen each which could buy a packet of French fries, a bun or a drink. Some days they packed food from home and were able to splurge on more expensive items on other days. Though we advised them not to buy junk food, we let them make their own decisions.

As they grew and their appetite increased (and inflation too!), we upped the allowance to one ringgit a day. For days when they had to stay back for tuition in school and had to eat lunch in the canteen, it was an additional ringgit for Yen Nee and two ringgit for Tze Wei who has twice the appetite of his younger sister.

Any savings from their school allowance is a mere pittance as it's just enough to cover food for recess and contribution for Sunday School.

When Pokemon cards became the rage, Tze Wei found an opportunity to augment his pocket money. He bought Pokemon cards which he sometimes exchanged with friends. One day he sold his cards to some friends who had offered to buy them. So he came up with the idea of buying Pokemon cards to sell for a profit.

My husband, seeing a business tycoon in the making, taught him the mechanics of trading. Tze Wei bought the cards in packs and sold them individually to his schoolmates, making profits ranging from 10 sen to 70 sen per card, depending on how badly the buyer wanted a particular card. He was happy to earn some money while the craze lasted but we warned him not to conduct his "business" during lesson time.

The children do have a regular source of "income"— their yearly *ang pow* money. When their collection totalled more than RM1,000 each, I opened a fixed deposit account for each of them. They were proud when they saw the FD certificates bearing their own names.

Their euphoria was shortlived as we had to cash their FDs when we were in a financial spot and needed every ringgit to pay our dues. We treated the money as a loan.

When the financial situation eased somewhat, my husband asked me to open a savings account for the children and bank in the money we owe them as well as their own periodic savings. I hesitated as I did not fancy the hassle of additional banking beyond the necessary obligation.

Instead, I issued two savings books from "mummy's bank" for Tze Wei and Yen Nee. I recorded the deposits from their *ang pows*, birthday gifts and examination rewards. In the four years that I've maintained these passbooks, there had only been a few withdrawals on their part. There was one withdrawal each for buying storybooks. There was a deduction in Tze Wei's passbook for upgrading the game boy his father bought for him as an examination incentive.

Other deductions recorded separately were donations to worthy causes. When our church had a special collection for the building fund, they dug into their *ang pow* money. When the Japanese Encephalitis crisis hit the pig farmers in Bukit Pelanduk, they donated from their savings. When their school passed the hat around for a cancer-stricken teacher, they took out money from their own pockets.

Hopefully by giving the children an early financial foundation, it will stand them in good stead when they are grown, so that they will know how to manage their money in a wise and circumspect manner.

1, 2, go

"**T**ZE WEI, go upstairs and do your homework," I said while preparing dinner in the kitchen.

The boy grunted but made no movement, his eyes glued to the television. He knew what I actually meant was, "You could go on watching until I check on you again."

Ten minutes later when I peeped into the living room, I saw that he hadn't budged an inch.

"Tze Wei, I thought I told you to do your homework." My voice had risen a few decibels. Translation: "It's okay, you've still got some time to watch."

"Yeah, yeah," he muttered absent-mindedly. He slowly rose from the sofa as a token of obedience.

I returned to the kitchen to prepare the fish for frying. When it was sizzling in the wok, I checked on the boy again. I found him perched on the one-seater, STILL watching TV.

"TZE WEI! I SAID—TO—GO—AND—DO —YOUR—HOMEWORK—NOW!!" I bellowed.

That was the ultimatum he was waiting for. He stomped off with a sulk that could turn milk into cheese.

If my husband were the one issuing the instruction, he would have gotten a prompt response. The kids know he means business. If he counted "one, two" and there was no response to his warning, they can be assured of the consequence that follows, whether it's a thwack from the cane or a tweak of the ear.

To them, Daddy's "one, two" means "go!" whereas Mummy's means "hang on, you've still got time until she gets really riled". It's my fault that they've got this perception. I'm not firm with them and they know they can get away with it sometimes. My five-year-old knows it only too well.

If I say, "Tze Ren, go wash up and get ready for bed," he might well ignore me. If I say, "one, two ..." but did not get up from where I was sitting, he would continue what he was doing without a flutter of the eyelid. If I say, "one ..." while getting up, he would make a move, eyes watching to see if I would reach for the cane on top of the piano. If I was side-tracked by the ringing phone or the baby, he knows he would get a reprieve. Once I got hold of the cane, he would scramble up the stairs post-haste.

Hubby knows my problem.

"Be consistent. Follow-up with your threat, don't let them get away with it," he says.

Actually I know that too but I have difficulty following through all the time. My niceness and leniency with the children tend to be taken advantage of. It can come to a stage where my words just bounce off them like little squash balls hitting the wall. Or I find myself repeating the same instructions over and over again like a broken record.

There will come a point when I simply cannot tolerate their nonchalance and I would explode in anger, giving them a severe tongue-lashing on respecting mummy and doing what she says pronto, or else .... After that they would be very obedient but would slip back into old habits if I become lax again.

One other thing which hubby always admonishes me to do is to give them some warning or notice if you please, instead of asking them to stop doing something immediately.

When we go swimming and if I ask the children to come out of the pool without any warning, they would invariably protest. But if I give them a grace period of say ten minutes, they wouldn't kick up a fuss when it's time to hit the shower.

If I want Tze Ren to keep his toys, instead of telling him to straightaway pack them up, he's more apt to cooperate if I say, "You have ten more minutes to play, after that you have to keep them." He gets additional time to play and is more willing to obey when the time is up. Of course, I have to follow-up in the designated time and issue a no-nonsense "one, two" so that he'd get up and go.

the instant pacifier

IF YOU WERE to tell my mother-in-law
that pacifiers cause babies' teeth to become crooked and
lips to be protruded, she would retort, "Nonsense! All my
children used the pacifier. Look at them, do they have
protruding lips and crooked teeth?"

She has something there. I think the pacifier has been
made a convenient scapegoat for imperfect genes. For me,
it is a very necessary mothering tool. In this day of instant
photographs and instant porridge, you could call it the
instant pacifier because it only takes an instance to pacify
fussy babies.

Granted there are other ways to soothe a crying baby
but the pacifier is a tried and tested one. Some children
take to sucking their thumbs to comfort themselves.
Between the pacifier and the thumb, I figure that the
former is the lesser evil. It would be easier to wean a child
off a pacifier than the thumb. With the pacifier, we simply
throw it away but we can't just cut off the thumb, can we?
After hearing how a friend had to put plaster and rub
chillies on her son's thumb to cure him of his
thumb-sucking, I'll rather stick to the pacifier, thank you
very much.

The pacifier—this four-syllable word is beginning to
sound klutzy, so I'll shorten it to Pessy—is a great friend to
babies and mothers. When my baby feels cranky or tired,

I simply pop Pessy into her mouth and she stops crying immediately. There are times when she just spits it out and continue crying but I'm happy if Pessy can do her job 70 per cent of the time.

Of course, when babies become too dependent on Pessy, it can lead to sticky situations, like the time we went for a holiday and I forgot to pack Pessy. My baby refused to take her nap and became extremely cranky. We had no choice but to drive to the nearest mini-market to buy another Pessy. Unfortunately, I couldn't find the same brand of Pessy that baby was using.

Babies can be so partial to their Pessy. It has to be just right—the same length, same roundness and the same feel. I picked one which fell literally short of her current Pessy. Well, something was better than nothing. I unwrapped the new Pessy, washed it and gave it to my watching baby. She sucked hard on it with a bemused expression which seemed to say, "My Pessy feels different," but she didn't spit it out. When we returned from the holiday, she switched to her old Pessy and refused to touch the new one.

My children are usually weaned off their Pessy when they are about 24 to 30 months old. It is a gradual process. As newborns, we let them have Pessy anytime they want. When they start to walk and learn how to talk, Pessy is reserved for cantankerous moments and naptime. Later we only let them have it when they sleep. The final step is letting them see Pessy thrown into the dustbin. When they hanker for it, we just tell them, "We've thrown it away." After a couple of days, Pessy would be totally forgotten.

Of course, there are times when it's hard for them to resist temptation. One occasion stands out vividly. My eldest child had been cured of Pessy addiction for some weeks. One day I went to pick him from my mum's. The front door was ajar. So I pushed it open. He was standing behind the door, sucking furiously on a Pessy. He knew he had been caught red-handed. Seeing guilt and remorse written all over his face, I didn't have the heart to reprimand him harshly. I removed Pessy from his mouth and gave him a mild ticking-off. Fortunately, that was the last time I've ever seen him with a Pessy.

So far I've not had any problems with the three older children when it is time to quit Pessy. The youngest is nineteen months old at the time of writing. Just the other night her Pessy went missing. She bawled her lungs out and refused to sleep. When I finally found Pessy and gave it to her, she immediately settled down to sleep. I hope she'll be able to kick her Pessy addiction without much difficulty later. Ah well, what's a few sleepless nights in exchange for more than 800 nights of peaceful slumber?

let the music play

EVERY evening, over the last two months, I've had the pleasure of listening to Richard Clayderman's "Ballade, Pour Adeline" being played by my neighbour's teenage daughter every evening while I prepared dinner. When I commented on her skilful playing to her mother, she said what almost every parent with a piano-playing child would say.

"I have to nag her to practise the piano. She thought of giving it up, but after spending so much money on lessons and the piano, how can we let her give it up so easily. In our days, we didn't have this opportunity at all. They're so lucky, but they don't realise it at all."

We're in the same boat. When Yen Nee was four we enrolled her in the Yamaha Junior Music Course (JMC). She enjoyed the classes and performed extremely well in the JMC examination.

When she graduated to the next level, trouble started. Lessons were conducted at a much faster pace. She was required to do more theory and practical work. She couldn't cope with the music homework as she also had tons of schoolwork.

Thinking that it might be better to let her learn at her own pace, we placed her in an individual piano class. We didn't pressure her unduly, yet she dragged her feet to the piano whenever we reminded her to practise. We even changed her teacher, thinking that perhaps her uninspiring style of teaching had something to do with her disinterest.

Still she didn't practise her pieces as she should and when she did, it was with a sullen face. It came to a point where she would only practise on the day of her music lesson. It was getting frustrating. We thought: why pay for her to practise at the music school when she should be practising at home and learning something new during the class? So we stopped her lessons when we moved to the other end of town.

"Get Yen Nee to practise the old pieces that she has learned," my husband suggested. "When she has picked up on her playing, we'll send her back for lessons." Easier said than done. I cajoled, I threatened, I reasoned with her. I ranted and raved. Nothing worked and it didn't achieve anything other than stressing us out, so I left her alone.

Then something happened. Last week she opened up the piano cover on her own accord, took out her music scores and played! Perhaps it had something to do with her little brother.

Lately two-and-a-half-year-old Tze Ren had been opening up the piano and tinkling with the keys. He does it properly too, with a music book propped up and both hands on the keys. I played a few nursery rhymes for him—"Mary had a Little Lamb", "London Bridge", and his favourite, "Twinkle, Twinkle, Little Star". He sang along. The words were gibberish but the tune was quite intact.

I think something must have stirred in Yen Nee when she saw Tze Ren enjoying the piano. I hope the interest that has been rekindled in her will keep on burning and that she will continue to play without prompting. Where nagging and needling had failed, example might have played a role in getting back the spark.

I am not sure what I will do if or when she becomes uninterested again. Maybe I should just sell the piano, recoup some of the cost and lower my blood pressure, all at one go. Maybe I should just let her discover her own interests at her own pace. Like they say, you can drag a horse to the water trough, but you can't force it to drink.

meet peter and jane

TZE WEI and Yen Nee started reading Peter and Jane books when they were four. The Montessori kindergarten they attended had a reading programme where the teachers taught the children to read at their own pace. There were 24 books in the series from Book 1A up to 12B. The children brought back their books every day to practice reading at home.

Progress was slow initially. It seemed to take forever for them to reach Book 4A. Sometimes our reading sessions went like this:

"This is Peter. This is Jane."

I yawned. This was going to be a long afternoon.

"Pam likes Jane and Jane likes Pam."

My eyelids started to droop.

"Pam sits with Jane in school."

My head nodded off.

"Jane and Peter are going to the farm for tea."

"Mummy, wake up!"

I felt a hand shaking my arm. I blinked my eyes to shake off the sleep.

"Mmmm ... Where are we now? Okay, you're here now? Let's continue reading."

"Here are the children at tea in the farm-house. Pam gives Peter some cakes."

"Cakes? Are you hungry? Let's go get something to eat," I suggested, glad for an excuse to get away from the dry and dreary book.

After book six, the speed picked up. Of course, the reward that came after each book was completed always spurred them on. It could be a toy, a stationery or a packet of chips.

The children soon whizzed through Books 7, 8 and 9 and before you could say "Pat the dog", they had finished the series. Okay-*lah*, I am exaggerating but in all, it took them about two years each to go through the 24 books.

Though reading about Peter, Jane and Pat's exploits is as exciting as watching grass grow, particularly on hot afternoons, I am thankful that they have taught my children to read.

When Tze Wei and Yen Nee had mastered the series, we returned the 24 Peter and Jane books to the kindergarten. I was glad I didn't have to read through them again.

Then Tze Ren came along. Last year, after much prodding from hubby, I started a half-hearted attempt to teach Tze Ren to read. The four-year-old wasn't ready for it and neither was I!

At the beginning of this year, I bought an entire set of Ladybird's Tom and Kate books, numbering 16 altogether. Having read through Peter and Jane twice is more than enough for a lifetime. Tze Ren and his little sister will get to know Tom, Kate and Sam instead.

Yen Nee, now eleven, leafed through the brand-new books and pronounced her verdict.

"Mmmm! Interesting."

"What did you think of the Peter and Jane books?" I asked 12-year-old Tze Wei.

"Can't remember. But I know it's veerrrryyy boring!" he said.

Compared to Peter and Jane, the Tom and Kate series appear to be more interesting. The illustrations are colourful and attractive. Even the stories are more appealing. As early as Book 2, dragons are introduced into the story. Book 3 paints pictures of castles and giants. Book 4 shows the silly antics of their pet dog, Sam.

As Tze Ren reads the words, his eyes darted through the pictures eagerly. After he reads through each page, I let him draw a star at the bottom to indicate that he's done with the page. After each book is completed, he gets a sticker award for the book. At the time of writing, he's on Book 8.

Though he still stumbles on words that he's already come across many times before like "then" or "these", I let him carry on with the rest of the page. As the reading scheme hinges on the "Look and Say" method, he'll come across them again and will learn them by and by.

Recently, my sister asked me to recommend a reading programme for her children. She and her husband run their own business and have no time to sit down to teach their children to read. Moreover, they are Chinese-educated and don't speak English fluently.

I checked out a popular phonics reading programme which charges RM80 per month and runs for about two years depending on the child's pace. The fees alone would come up to about RM2,000. And there are separate charges for reading materials and workbooks.

I told my sister about my children's success with the Ladybird series but as she doesn't have the time, isn't proficient in English and doesn't mind burning a hole in her pocket for her children, I suggested that she go ahead with the phonics reading programme.

As for me, I'd rather plod through the books. They're effective and economical, a winning combination, if I may say so.

independence milestones

IN OUR CHILDREN'S LIVES, various milestones mark the different levels of independence they attain at different points in time.

When they are toilet-trained, we jump with joy.

When they could bathe themselves, that's a feather in the cap.

When they go to nursery school and could alight from the car without kicking a fuss, we grin from ear to ear.

When they start Year 1 in primary school and forget all about your presence the minute they see their friends, we beam with pride.

When they sleep over at a friend's place or go for an overnight school trip, we feel the loosening of apron strings.

When they don their secondary school uniforms, we marvel at how mature they look.

When they decide to be baptised, we rejoice with the angels in heaven.

Every child is different, each with his own characteristics which can be as unique as his fingerprints. And they all develop at different paces and achieve their independence milestones at differing points in their lives.

Tze Wei, my eldest, was a timid boy. When we sent him to kindergarten at four, he cried for a week. I did not linger in school after dropping him off and he soon stopped crying after I left.

When it came to Yen Nee's turn the following year, she didn't have separation anxiety as her brother was around. Six years later, Tze Ren the extrovert didn't even notice me after I deposited him in class.

My two older kids are by nature more reserved than number three who's always rearing to go. I remember an incident when Tze Wei was three or four. It was during a Sunday School outdoor programme. I had to organise the children into groups, brief them on the rules, get the props in position and conduct the games. So you could imagine my agitation as the boy was literally hanging on to my pants and getting in the way. Despite giving him a stern talking-to, he was still velcroed to me

Fast forward a few years to one particular Chinese New Year when a group of about twenty people visited our home. We didn't have enough ice for the large number of visitors, so I asked Tze Wei to buy ice from the sundry shop behind our house. It was a very short distance, turn two corners and you're there. That was to be the eight-year-old's first errand out of the house, all on his own.

Call me paranoid but my motherly instinct feared for the safety of my son. It's not like our younger days where children could play safely outside the house without fear of criminals abducting them or cars running over them. These are different times we live in. Hardly a day passes by without us reading of murders, kidnappings, rapes, burglaries or accidents. I whispered a prayer for him as I sent him off and breathed a sigh of relief when he returned safely.

Tze Ren started running errands at a younger age. No, I didn't send the five-year-old to the shops on his own. I would drive up to a grocer's and ask him to buy a loaf of bread while I wait in the car. He would walk to the bread rack, pick up a loaf of bread and on seeing my nod indicating that he's got the right product, go in and pay the shopkeeper. He always returns with a grin at his accomplishment.

He's so independent and brave that he could be lost in a departmental store and not be scared. Recently I went shopping with him. He was dashing all over the place while I browsed. While paying for my purchase I noticed that he was missing. I retraced my steps and found him near the entrance, his head turning left and right in search of me. When he saw me, he came running with a big smile on his face, saying "I was looking for you." No tears and no fears for this boy who kept asking, "Mummy, what must I eat to become eleven?"

LEISURELY PURSUITS

the stress of countless contests

WHEN I FLIP through any newspaper or magazine, nine times out of 10, I would come across a contest promising prizes galore. From six-digit cash prizes to electrical appliances, from holiday cruises to meal vouchers, these goodies tempt consumers to buy those products to enter the contests.

Visions of a bulging bank account or cruising around in a gleaming four-wheel-drive never fail to reach out their tentacles and entice me to contribute towards the contest organisers' coffers, unless they require a preposterous proof of purchase like buying an expensive electrical appliance, an air ticket or in some cases even a spanking new car. I think that would be an ultimate case of sen-wise, ringgit foolish unless I happen to be shopping around for a sleek sedan which is most unlikely as I am cash strapped until I win that cash prize. Vicious circle this.

Most contests require contestants to answer a couple of simple questions which any kid could tackle with his eyes closed. Of course, they, they meaning contest organisers, cannot make the contest too difficult, otherwise consumers would not buy their products to enter the contest.

Occasionally, they make you work for your prize. There was this contest where participants have to count the zillions of tiny animals on the contest form. It was a tough assignment. The paper was crawling with beetles, foxes, bears and squirrels. And they were everywhere, on treetops, on car tops, behind rocks, on leafs, under the waterfall.

That was one contest I didn't want to enter—until one hot night when sleep eluded me. Instead of tossing in bed and counting sheep, which did not lull me to sleep, I decided to count minuscule beetles, foxes, bears and squirrels to earn myself a 4WD.

I formulated a foolproof strategy. Armed with a magnifying glass and pencil, I divided the paper into eight squares. I counted the animals square by square and managed to add them all up by five in the morning.

After submitting my form, I waited for the call to claim my 4WD. I was still patiently waiting when I saw a picture of the winner published in the newspaper. She was a demure-looking Malay lady, beaming as she received a giant-sized replica of the car key. Poof! My dream car vanished like vapour.

Being the positive thinker that I am, I pushed that incident into an obscure corner of my memory bank until my bank ran a contest where they promised a holiday at any destination I wanted. Never mind that I can't have the 4WD. After all I already have a car. No doubt it's old, no doubt it's not swanky but I can get around in town. But I need the bank to pay those air tickets to Bali, my island in the sun for my dream holiday.

To qualify for the contest, participants must attach 10 ATM transaction slips. This did not pose any problem except that only ATM slips with the words "Win a great holiday" printed on them would qualify for the contest.

And not every slip that spewed out from the ATM slot had this coveted phrase.

I had already collected six slips in the past few months and only needed four more. The closing date was looming close so I needed a grand plan. This was it: I would make a special trip to the bank and repeatedly withdraw RM50 until I have the required number of slips. After a few withdrawals, I got the hang of how their system worked.

The first transaction slip would be blank; the next would be a "free tissue box" slip, which entitled you to 100 pieces of free tissue, followed by another blank slip. The fourth one would be the "Win a great holiday" slip! Well done, Nancy Drew.

I got all my ten slips, half a dozen of free tissue boxes and at the end of the month, an additional page of bank statement which listed all those RM50 withdrawals. The contest came and went, but the bank still had not called me with the wonderful news of my winning. Sigh, it looked like I had to bid farewell to Bali before I can even set foot on it. All the hard work and slogging at the slogan—for nothing.

Sometimes I take many hours just to coin one catchy slogan. Other times when practicality reigns, I just scribble whatever comes to mind. After all I don't expect them to open 5,000 envelopes and peruse 5,000 slogans, 90 per cent of which would probably be badly written. It is more likely they would do a lucky draw on the mountain of entries and then only use the slogan to decide on the winners.

Nowadays, there's a new contest format that does away with the writing of slogans. The idea is to sign the product name in the most creative manner and voila, you could be the proud owner of that bag of cash or double storey house.

It's amazing how many variations can be done with one word. I tried my hand at such a contest this year and wasted maybe two trees in the process. I thought I was being clever when I finally fashioned the product name into a rabbit, this being the Year of the Rabbit. Obviously they did not think so as my name did not appear in the list of winners published. But then again, it might be that my entry was buried 20,000 leagues under that ocean of entries.

There's a new kid on the block: the contest which does not require any slogan writing or signing. What is needed is a wallet full of cash, to purchase their product. The more, the better. The winner is the one who submitted the receipt with the highest purchase.

I shudder when I imagine this scenario. I buy one RM1,000 worth of underwear to win that grand prize of RM1,500. After all, I still get RM500 profit when I win the booty. On D-day, I discover that the winner is the lady who totals RM1,400 on one receipt. What?! No prize and a cupboard full of underwear? I may give them away as presents (if they fit the recipients) but on second thought, I'd better not. My friends may think that contest mania had twisted my mind.

dial that number!

"QUICK! Dial the number now!" I said as I lobbed the handphone to my son.

The cue to call for the radio contest had come on while I was sending my boy to school. He kept dialling the number without success, which wasn't surprising considering that maybe six million people were jamming the line. After all, RM5,000 was at stake. People have been known to dial off their fingers for a CD pack, what more this stash of cash which keeps snowballing if there is no correct answer?

This particular contest was called the Ultimate Ear Test where callers had to guess what a given sound was. Usually the biggest challenge in radio contests is getting your call through and when you do, you have to be the designated number of caller, whether it's the first, fifth, ninth or whatever.

In this contest, not only have you got to be among the first three callers, you had to guess what the sound was, which was like asking a toddler what Einstein's theory of relativity is. Of course, every now and then, a very lucky genius who managed to get through the eternally busy line would come along and swipe the bountiful booty.

No, it's not easy winning a radio contest. Timing is everything. Grab the phone a split second too late, and you can dial till the cows come home and still not get through. Dial too early, and you'll be elated to hear a ringing tone (at long last!) and the deejay saying, "Second caller, please try again," when you want to be the 24th caller.

Once in a blue moon, in that millionth of a second after a listener has ended his call, your call happens to connect at that precise moment and you get through! If the deejay picks up your call in another ongoing contest called the Mix Six, you could end up with—are you ready for this— RM60,000! That's six years' salary for some people.

All you have to do is identify the stipulated six songs that have been played back-to-back. Easy peasy. That is, if you can freeze six million hands in the midst of punching that number.

Sometimes getting through to the station doesn't always mean a big prize awaits. You can count on the sponsors to come up with interesting ways to make that elusive bounty more slippery than an eel to grasp.

Earlier this year I did manage to call in at that millionth-of-a-second moment. I had heard the cue to call while negotiating through lunch-time traffic, dialled the number on my handphone and what do you know? I was the successful eighth caller!

Contestants were given a choice of cash or the red box in the *Ang Pow* or Red Box contest. The deejay would tempt the caller with three different cash values, starting off with say, RM100 and rising to maybe RM800. The contestant could choose the cash or if he was adventurous, go for the mysterious red box which could contain anything from a packet of melon seeds to the key to a brand-new Atos.

In my case I was offered a measly final sum of RM160. Of course, I went for the red box. If I had been offered RM800 I might just have grabbed the cash instead of hoping the car key would be in the box. So what did I win? A pair of hand-me-down sunglasses from one of the deejays!

Suddenly RM160 seemed like an awful lot of money. I could have bought 80 loaves of bread with that amount. Never mind. One little bun is better than none.

But I've won a grand prize before. It was during a Secretaries Week contest held two years ago. A fitting prize, I might say, as I worked as a secretary previously. Contestants had to take a short dictation and read it back to the deejay. The caller with the most number of correct words would win a luxurious hotel stay worth RM3,000 on top of the regular prize of two tickets to Anita Sarawak's show.

After a few unsuccessful tries, I eventually managed to become the fifth caller. I was so nervous I was hyperventilating. Hearing myself on the radio later, I sounded like I was gasping for breath after climbing up the stairs to Batu Caves. That didn't matter.

What did was that I only made three mistakes out of 27 words, the best score at that time and as it turned out, for the duration of the contest. I still remember the deejay's words, "You're a shining example to your previous profession."

Having said that, I'm no pro at radio contests. My brother-in-law is. He loves to take part in trivia contests and has won many prizes. This is his modus operandi. His son dials on one phone, his maid on the fax line (he works from home) while he looks up the answer in the encyclopaedia. He has won hotel vouchers, electrical appliances, and lots of other stuff I don't know about. No doubt the value of the prize can't beat that RM60,000 up for grabs now, but often it's not the quantum that matters. It's the thrill of winning something that gives the adrenaline rush, which is why people will continue to call in for those CD packs.

"Son! Dial that number! It's the cue to call!"

watch it, auntie!

AS A TEENAGER I often tagged along with my auntie and neighbour for their regular jaunts at the cinema. The staple in the 1970s was Taiwanese romance movies where the two Chins, Charlie Chin and Chin Han, and two Lins, Lin Chin Hsia and Lin Fong Chiao, dominated the silver screen.

Going to the movies then was such a different experience from what it is today. There was no telephone reservation for advance booking. If it was a blockbuster movie, we had to go a day earlier to purchase tickets. Otherwise, we could be caught in a long queue.

Sometimes a brawl might ensue when impatient men clamber over each other to get to the ticket counter for choice seats.

At the counter you didn't have to ask what seats were available as the seat layout was spread out in front of the cashier. Seats sold would have been crossed out with a red pencil.

We usually purchased ground-floor tickets as the balcony section was rather expensive. Our order of preference was back row seats followed by the middle section and occasionally we even settled for the tiresome neck-craning front rows, which were the cheapest of the lot. If I remember correctly, it was only 65 sen which was dirt cheap in those days.

The moviegoing experience would not have been complete without making a stop at the various stalls selling munchies at the cinema foyer and premises outside. Snacks ranged from papaya and *ciku* to melon seeds and preserved fruits, peanuts and crackers to soya bean and black jelly drinks. The wide variety of food available meant more rubbish was scattered. At the end of each show, the floor looked like a garbage-strewn street after a *pasar malam* (night market) was over.

Unlike today's cineplexes with terraced stadium seating, cinema seats then were on a sloping level. That didn't do much for a shortie like me. When someone tall sat in front of me, I had to play musical chairs with my companions unless the tallie in front slouched on his chair. Honestly, those wooden seats were not kind on the posture and posterior.

When the lights came on and everybody stood up, the wooden seats snapped back into vertical position, producing a chorus of clack-clack-clackity-clack like rapidly tumbling giant dominoes.

Back then there was no state-of-the-art sound system. There wasn't anything memorable about it except for the loud whirring sound of the projector as the film unrolled. Acoustics were lousy. There was no thick carpeting to muffle noises. The sound of the audience snacking was magnified in the enclosed hall.

As the trailers unfold, the splitting of melon seeds, munching of crackers and rustling of food wrappers filled the hall. When somebody wearing heels walked down the aisle, she went click-click-clickety-click on the cement floor all the way to the toilet. As the thick curtains to the toilet was pushed aside, a shaft of bright light from the toilet beamed into the darkened auditorium.

Nowadays, if you see someone with a sweater slung across her shoulders in a shopping mall housing a cineplex, chances are she'll be watching a movie there.

These days, moviegoers do not need a scary show to raise their goosepimples; the super efficient air-conditioning could do that very well, thank you. In yonder years you toted a sweater only if you were going to Genting Highlands or Fraser's Hill, never to a cinema where you could sweat buckets when the rickety air-con went kaput or when you caught the last show of the night during which the air-con was switched off midway.

Occasionally we would catch an afternoon matinee. What I disliked about daytime jaunts had something to do with cinema exit doors opening out into the glare of the daylight. After the customary darkness, the dazzling sunlight caused giddiness and a momentary loss of bearing. Thank goodness for the subdued lighting in modern cineplexes where our eyes will not be subjected to the sudden assault of bright lights when the credits roll.

Technology has certainly heightened the spills and thrills of movies today but having warmed the seats of many a majestic stand-alone cinemas of old, I would say that the moviegoing experience of days yonder had its share of excitement, albeit of a different nature.

the magical wand

I'M A FROG under the coconut shell when it comes to the finer things in life. I'm your average Ah Moi who derives more pleasure from the radio's music selection than the likes of Mozart and Beethoven. Similarly my husband is your everyday Ah Chong who's more apt to listen to the Bee Gees than Tchaikovsky.

So when my sister-in-law invited us for an orchestra performance at the Dewan Filharmonik Petronas, we accepted with a little trepidation. But if her husband, who had been a reluctant spectator, had acquired the taste for classical concerts, it's likely that we could learn to appreciate it too.

I was surprised to see a packed hall. Everyone seemed to be appropriately dressed for the Sunday matinee which had a dress code of smart casual. The crowd was dignified. Conversation was muted. The middle-aged made up the majority with a sprinkling of young people in their 20s. Punctuality is a prerequisite unless one fancies being locked out of the hall until the next interval which could be a good half hour.

My husband and I were seated at the back of the auditorium while my sister-in-law and her husband sat somewhere in front as she couldn't get four tickets in a row. The premium seats are located in the middle section

240

which offers the best view and where the full impact of the music can be heard.

Despite their expensive price tag, these choice seats are always snapped up way in advance. I feel sorry for spectators seated on the first row. They have to content themselves with looking at the shoes and trouser legs of the performers unless they crane their necks for a better view.

Right on the dot at 3.00p.m., the lights in the audience section went out. The musicians, I counted 63, trooped onto the stage. They settled down on their chairs and tested their instruments. A flurry of music arose as the sounds of violins, cellos, trombones and horns collided with one another.

But this died down quickly. That was the cue for the conductor to enter. He took his place at the conductor's platform in front of the stage. There was no doubt about it. Mr. Conductor was the star of the show. He was the hand that pieced together 63 pieces of jigsaw puzzle into one big picture.

I wouldn't have thought that looking at a man's back could be so mesmerising. One moment he was swaying gracefully like willows in the breeze, the next he was like a tree bending in a thunderstorm. Now he was flicking his fingers towards his nose. Then he was gesticulating wildly with his wand as if he was beating a dog.

Sometimes he swung his arm backwards as if doing the back crawl. Occasionally one hand shot backwards to grab the railing in front of the platform as if he needed its support while he pranced around.

Mr. Conductor reminded me of a Bugs Bunny cartoon I once watched. I don't mean that as an affront to the conductor but as a salute to Warner Bros' animators. They have captured the very essence of a musical conductor, right down to its minutest mannerism. In the cartoon, Bugs Bunny starred as the musical conductor whose actions were being replayed live before my very eyes. Even the part where Mr. Conductor's feet seemed to be plastered to the platform as he swung forward from side to side invoked a *déjà-vu* feeling.

I was told later that not all conductors display such energetic performances. There are those who can easily turn on the snooze button for the audience. I'm glad we caught this orchestra instead of another, otherwise we might have dropped off at dreamland.

The other performer who stole the thunder was the drummer. In a sea of violinists, cellists, horn and trombone musicians, the odd drummer was bound to command attention. Besides, he put up a dazzling performance. With four drums laid out before him, he was quick to swivel from left to right to left again, changing drumsticks midway too. Nimble is the word to describe him.

At one point, there was a pause long enough to make me wonder if the piece had ended. It was so quiet you could hear a feather drop. To clap or not to clap, that is the question that plagues the novice spectator. The answer is simple. Follow the crowd and you won't go wrong.

When the piece eventually ended, the crowd erupted into rapturous applause. We clapped too but not as enthusiastically as my neighbour who clapped so hard her shoulders danced.

The applause remained unabated for a good five minutes during which the conductor took his bow, went backstage, came out again and motioned for the musicians to stand up group by group. When the drummer stood up to take his bow, whoops of cheer greeted him. Clearly he was the audience's favourite.

There and then my perception that Malaysian spectators are an unappreciative bunch was dashed against the warm wooden wall panelling of Dewan Filharmonik Petronas. If I were at the receiving end of such applause, I would have cried.

COUCH POTATOES

spanish soap fever

HOUSEWIVES watch them. Civil servants close their counters to view them. Lecturers rush home from college to catch them. And students put aside their books to see them. Yep, those Spanish language soap operas churned out by the Latin American countries have Malaysians firmly in their grip.

All our TV stations are helping to spread the fever. There's *El Amor No Es Como Lo Pintan* on TV2, *La Intrusa* on TV3 and *Juana's Miracle* and the rerun of *Mis Tres Hermanas* on NTV7.

What is it about these Spanish soaps that propel viewers to their TV sets every weekday afternoon following the twists and turns in the protagonists' lives?

For me, the addiction started with Maria Mercedes three years ago. It was a fresh change from the ubiquitous Hong Kong serials that were the staple at that time. I was sick of *kung fu* epics with its ridiculous stunts and the crass dialogue of modern-day dramas.

I was ready for something culturally different. I wanted to see the Latin American's way of life set amidst an intriguing background of family squabbles and black mail, stolen kisses and betrayal, all amply available in its soap operas.

It is undeniable that good looks is a major factor in drawing the audience. With beautiful stars gracing the

screen such as Thalia Sodi Miranda in *Rosalinda*, Gabriela
Spanic in *La Intrusa* and Ricardo Alamo in *Juana's Miracle*,
the battle for viewers' hearts is half won. They are a
delight to watch. In our mundane everyday lives, there are
plenty of ordinary-looking folks around. These ravishing
thespians are iced cakes amidst a spread of hawker food.

But looks alone will not sustain the soap. It's also
buoyed by the actors' realistic portrayal of their
characters. In *Betty Yo Soy La Fea*, Ana Maria Orozco
played Betty so well that we felt hurt when she was
slighted for her homeliness. When her boss with whom
she had fallen in love betrayed her, we plunged into the
bottomless pit with her.

Jorge Enrique Abello's performance as the playboy
boss made us want to slap him for his shabby treatment of
Betty but in his hour of remorse, we rooted for him.

The stories run the gamut from run-of-the-mill
formula of boy-meets-girl, fall in love, encounter
obstacles and eventually love conquers all as in *Rosalinda*,
to the highly imaginative tale of a 17-year-old virgin
being artificially inseminated by mistake in *Juana's Miracle*.

However, at the centre of each yarn is a common
thread. More often than not the main character is a
woman, who besides being beautiful and buxom, is also
humble and vulnerable. She hits rock bottom at some
point but will rise through the ashes like the legendary
phoenix and eventually win her man.

This brings me to the next point. The male
protagonists are usually portrayed as full of flaws. In *La
Usurpadora*, the husband of the heroine finds himself
falling in and out of love at the drop of a pin. One day he
loves his sexy wife but the next day he is attracted to his

secretary. Then he falls for a woman he met on a holiday. It makes you want to shake him and shout, "Make up your mind, you fickle-minded Don Juan!" In *Maria Mercedes*, the hero is an indecisive mummy's boy, and in *Betty*, the hot-tempered playboy boss.

There is also the mandatory romance in the *tele-novelas*. In every series, the flame of love burns bright in the heroin's heart. What did they say about love making the world go round? It certainly makes the soaps spin.

Like reading a well-written novel that keeps you turning the pages, Spanish soaps keep you tuning in to find out the story's progress. Usually the pace keeps viewers at the edge of their seats but there are times when it is as slow-moving as a bumper-to-bumper crawl on the Federal Highway. Missing an episode or two doesn't mean you'll lose out on a lot of action. You can still piece together the events. Just make sure you're parked in front of the telly for exciting moments like when Betty undergoes her transformation from an ugly duckling to a pretty woman or when the villain in *Mis Tres Hermanas* was about to blow his brains out after his wicked scheming is exposed.

Whatever it is, these dramas have snared viewers hook, line and sinker for the long haul of over 150 episodes per serial.

TV stations usually air the *tele-novelas* in Spanish. I prefer this to having it dubbed in Malay. Dubbed dialogue somehow loses the emotions and nuances portrayed by the actors. Besides we don't seem to have a large pool of voice talents in Malaysia. Invariably every dubbed show has Doraemon's voice in it. It is hard to take Maria

Mercedes seriously when she sounds like a cartoon character.

This means that viewers have to depend on subtitles to understand the show. Fortunately, our translators are doing a better job these days. I remember a time when "fire!" as in shooting a gun was translated as *"api"* and "freeze!" as in don't move appearing as *"beku"*. Such *faux pas* is a thing of the past. Still, there's the frustration of having one miserable subtitle summing up lines of dialogue, making viewers more bemused instead of enlightened.

The day I discovered that Spanish soaps have a large following was when Ntv7 inadvertently left out the subtitles for an episode of *La Usurpadora*. I immediately called up the station but the line was busy. When I finally got through, the telephone operator apologised for the oversight before I could even voice my complaint. So there were others like myself who are wondering what the police chief was saying to Paulina Martinez as he was about to apprehend the heroine in *La Usurpadora*.

The benefit of watching Spanish soaps is that I'm able to pick up a smattering of Spanish (at least I won't feel guilty for spending so much time in front of the television). Though the knowledge is insufficient for conversing, I could greet my *mi amor* with *Buenos Dias*, before asking him to *por favor* give me some *dinero*. If he doesn't hand it over, I'll ask him *por qu* and if he doesn't give a good reason, I'll chase him out of *mi casa*. For non-Spanish soap fans, the translated phrases in order of appearance are my love, Good Morning, please, money, why, my house. Get it?

Besides documentaries and news, tell me which TV programme is not a means of escapism? Whether kicking butt with Sydney Bristow in *Alias* or rolling around grassy plains ... la Bollywood, TV shows enable us to escape into a realm not inhabited by mundane denizens. Same with Spanish soaps.

For an hour a day (or more if you watch more than one soap), we could flee into the make-believe world where melodrama and romance, intrigue and suspense cast their spell on us. Then it's back to cooking dinner or manning the counters, marking assignments or doing homework.

As a stay-at-home mum who has access to the TV anytime of the day, if I didn't exercise some discipline, I could well be watching three hours of Latin American *tele-novelas* every day. I don't have enough laundry to fold or gingko nuts to crack to justify three hours in front of the TV. Not even if I were to take up my mother-in-law's suggestion of dusting the shelves while watching my favourite drama. I'll just have to take my pick or I'll go *loca* with Spanish soap fever. That means crazy, get it?

versatile mr. subtitles

OUR TV programmes are more kaleidoscopic than our multiracial composition of Malays, Chinese, Indian and others. Besides Malay, Mandarin, Cantonese, Hindi and Tamil, there's Spanish, Korean, Japanese, Arabic, Tagalog, Thai, Indonesian and the ubiquitous English programmes. Therefore it is inevitable that viewers have to rely on subtitles to understand the numerous foreign-language programmes unless they have been dubbed into a language understood by locals.

Even if one is conversant in a particular tongue, subtitles do come in handy when lines are spoken too fast or mangled by foreign accent. Like the Mr. Men's series of books by British author Roger Hargreaves, TV programmes subtitles can be personified by their characteristics. Read on to find out who they are.

Mr. Literal

This chap has gone into hiding. He used to give comedies a run for their money. Remember a time when "fire" was translated as *api* instead of *tembak* and "freeze" was *beku*, not *berhenti*. That's Mr. Literal. He used to do wonders for facial muscles. Not anymore.

The present crop of subtitle writers don't do direct translations anymore. That's so passé. Nowadays they translate everything in context.

When I heard this line from *Asteroid*, "You're pulled in ten different directions", I thought I was going to get a glimpse of Mr. Literal appearing as *"Awak ditarik ke sepuluh hala yang berlainan."* But no, what came out was *"Awak membuat banyak kerja pada masa yang sama."* It's no fun anymore. I guess I'll have to depend on sitcoms to exercise those facial muscles.

Mr. Overlapping

Sometimes a movie or serial may come with Chinese and English subtitles. For programmes in Chinese, I prefer to read the Chinese subtitles in order to improve my Mandarin. Besides I find them pretty precise and detailed, right down to every sigh and groan. That's why I detest it when the Malay subtitles overlap the Chinese and English ones.

Instead of imposing Mr. Overlapping on us, why don't the TV stations give viewers the choice of three languages? That way, if one wants to learn English, they've got the English subtitles to help them. Ditto for Chinese and Malay.

And what better way to learn a language? It's entertainment and education at one go. That's how I picked up my Mandarin, not in a Chinese school but from the movies.

Mr. Bombastic

This guy seldom makes an appearance but when he does, you wouldn't know what hit you. In an episode of *Alias*, translations such as *taksub* appeared though not many were wiser on what it meant. (The word actually means obsessed.) In the Chinese serial, *Leung Shan Pak and Juliet*,

the words *"jual tembaga"* cropped up in the subtitles but
there was no hint of anyone selling copper in the show.

Mr. Respectful

He appears as *"terima kasih, ayah"* when a son says "Thank
you" to his father. Or when someone is talking to an elder
who is not a relative, he butts in as *"pakcik"* or *"makcik"*
though there's no uncle or aunty mentioned in the
dialogue.

Mr. Cultural Context

If someone says, "You rat!" in an American movie, that
can't be translated as *"Awak tikus!"* as that would give a
different connotation. In the English context, a rat
denotes a scoundrel but *tikus* implies filth. Mr. Cultural
Context would turn up as *Kau bangsat!*

Similarly "Doctor Frankenstein" may have viewers
scratching their heads if they haven't heard of the creator
of the green-faced, flat-headed monster but *Doktor Syaitan*
is universally understood.

Mr. No-Show Coz He's Too Polite

Our censors would have ensured that all obscenities have
been bleeped out so there's no worry that "my ass" or "son
of a bitch" would appear as *punggung saya* or *anak anjing
betina*. But what about coarse language which doesn't
border on the obscene but is jarring on the ears?

That would be Mr. No-Show. To illustrate: in the
Mother's Day special movie, *Mrs. Winterbourne*, the
foul-mouthed protagonist scolded the maid who wanted
to take her baby from her arms. "No! He doesn't have his

teats right on hand." Realising her faux pas (she's in the company of distinguished folks), she said, "Oops, sorry. I mean breasts." I'm certain that wouldn't be translated as *Tidak! Dia perlukan tetek saya pada bila-bila masa. Maafkan saya, maksud saya, dada.* That would be too crude. It could actually be a sanitised, *"Tidak, saya perlu menyusunya pada bila-bila masa,"* but the subtitle writer decided to bring in Mr. No-Show.

Mr. Absent Coz He's Too Funny

Trying to translate jokes is like attempting to float a car with helium. That's why I'd rather not watch a comedy if I don't understand the language spoken. More often than not the punch line is lost in the translation or the rib-tickling parts entirely omitted. That's where Mr. Absent comes in.

A case in point from *Everybody Loves Raymond*. When Raymond's dad was rambling about the German Shepherds, you thought he was talking about dogs until he said, "Those days the Germans were protective of their territory." Even Raymond had a hard time keeping a straight face.

Is it any wonder then that the subtitle writer avoided the line as if it's infected with the SARS virus? And how would you translate "your grandma has hit the sauce"? *Nenek awak telah menghentam kuah?* Oops! I forgot. Literal translations are a no-no. That's why Mr. Absent is indispensable.

Mr. Missing-in-Action

Here's a scene from a Bollywood movie. The hero's mum was talking and gesturing wildly. Hero said something.

Mum slapped him, uttering something at rapid fire speed. Hero's girlfriend interjected and stopped another blow from mum. Mum broke down in tears.

All this has been going on sans subtitles. The only words I understood were "*aiyoyo*" and "*amma*". The rest of the conversation could as well have been Hebrew for all the sense it made.

Mr. Missing-In-Action sure makes me feel frustrated, like Shah Rukh Khan throwing punches at Salman Khan but missing. Now, I understand that essence is the crux of the matter, but it's the little extras that enhance appreciation of a show.

Mr. Forgotten

I'll never forget when the Spanish soap *La Usupadora* was aired without subtitles at a crucial moment. The police inspector was about to apprehend the heroine Paulina Martinez who was impersonating as Paola Bracho. He called "Paulina Martinez!" from behind her. She turned around to face him. Uh-oh, she's in trouble! She's supposed to be Paola Bracho, how could she respond to the name of Paulina?

Thanks to Mr. Forgotten, I'll never know how she talked her way out of that predicament as the subtitles only appeared in the next scene.

That episode taught me not to take subtitles for granted. They're an integral part of television viewing, especially for foreign-language programmes. They're like the pedals of a bicycle. Without them, you ain't going nowhere.

Take a bow, Mr. Subtitles.

mouldy oldies

"YOU'D better stay away from those computers. They can make you sterile."

This whopper came out of the mouth of Mike Hammer during the midnight rerun of the 1980s series of the same name. My head was nodding like a Raggedy Ann doll with a limp neck but it jerked right up when I heard that line. What a joke! Sure the eighties was the dark ages when 286 computers and monochrome monitors ruled the offices but Mike's warning was as lame as the wet towel he wore in one episode.

My first instinct was right about Mike Hammer. I didn't like the show when it first ran in the 1980s. I don't like it now. It's too sexist. Women were portrayed as bimbos with their bountiful assets popping out of low-cut outfits, ready to seduce the hero at the drop of a hat in every episode. It's disgusting. I'm not the only one who feels this way. A friend of mine who had the misfortune to tune in to the show shares the same sentiment. Both of us think that Mike Hammer ought to be cold-storaged.

Midnight TV viewing is not the norm for me. It's usually reserved for *Survivor* and *The Amazing Race* which are convoluted enough to keep me awake. But the insipid adventures of a moustachioed investigator overloaded on testosterone lull me to sleep faster than I can count sheep.

Thankfully the reruns of the other oldie action series, *Charlie's Angels* and *Knight Rider* aren't as loathsome though I have to prop up my eyelids with toothpicks in order to sit through the shows. I grew up watching them in the 1970s and 1980s but I've outgrown them. Just moving with the times. You see, action series don't age like wine the way sitcoms or dramas do. One can watch Samantha Stevens twitch her nose in *Bewitched* or Laura Ingalls' charming, fascinating adventures in *Little House on the Prairie* without that cheesy feeling. Even cowboy flicks such as *Rawhide* or *Bonanza* come across as old-world charm.

One word describes oldie action series. Flat. Like overnight Pepsi. By comparison, today's action flicks are like Pepsi Blue—funky and fizzy. There's nothing wrong with these oldies but if you must, blame it on progress. Twenty years pack a whole bunch of innovation and quantum leap in technology that had a great impact in the reel world. From the evolvement of computers to mobile phone culture, these have made their mark on TV shows.

Computers are used to create all manner of special effects like the silvery droplets of liquid that bathes over the hero whenever he's about to vanish in *The Invisible Man* series of the new millenneum. David McCallum's 1970s version which saw him shedding his coat, hat, gloves and finally unraveling the long scarf that cloaked his invisibility can now be relegated to the museum.

And take a look at the cars. In the 1980s, *Knight Rider's* black Pontiac Trans Am looked sleek and sporty. Now it has an old junk appearance, like a beat-up car destined to crash in a B-grade movie. The 21st-century spanks of SUVs, MPVs, aerodynamic super saloons and ultra-modern James Bondian sports cars.

In *Knight Rider*, KITT the talking car was a piece of state-of-the-art equipment complete with computer that can pick up surrounding noises, scan its database for information on suspects and impress pretty damsels hanging on the arms of Michael Knight. Today only a grandmother who hasn't seen sophisticated computers would be bowled over by KITT. Its square computer screen is so phony it's almost embarrassing.

Everybody owns a mobile phone nowadays. It isn't the luxury it used to be. For crime fighters, it's a tool that ranks up there with their weapon. Can you imagine the modern detective looking around for a public phone to call the police for back-up? That was exactly what the 1970s' *Charlie's Angels* did. They used the public phone and walkie-talkies to keep tabs with one another.

If Sabrina Duncan, Jill Munroe and Kelly Garrett could travel in a time machine to the 21st century and see their fellow angels in action in the movie version, they would have gone ga-ga with the high-tech gadgets and dare-devil stunts. Though the original angels were considered as tough cookies in their time, these cookies have gone soft with the winds of change. The 1970s' baddies weren't as violent as the modern breed. A chop on the shoulder or a couple of bowling balls thrown in the right direction would overpower them quite easily.

The new crop of action heroines such as Xena, Nikita and *Alias*'s Sydney Bristow can sing Carl Douglas's "Kung Fu Fighting" and mean it. The lyrics go like this: "Everybody was kung fu fighting. Hee! Hah! Those kids were fast as lightning, in fact it was a little bit frightening, but they fought with expert timing."

These gals can perform flying kicks and somersaults
and judo-chop muscular men into a crumpled heap on the
floor. One look at Sydney's sinewy body and you know
you won't want to mess with her. Some of these actresses
are exponents of martial art but even if they aren't, they're
required to undergo vigorous training to lend authenticity
to the feisty roles.

Where action is concerned, plain fist fighting doesn't
chalk up much entertainment value anymore. Legwork
figures a lot in the newer action flicks. Scissors kick,
running up the wall and what-have-you are part of the
nifty action choreography designed to captivate viewers'
interests. In *Martial Law*, Samo Hung's fast-paced action
scenes reminiscent of Jackie Chan's dodge-them style and
use of unlikely props is both comical and entertaining.
Juxtapose that with Mike Hammer's brawl with the
baddies and you'd agree that Mike has become dull with
the passage of time.

Another reason for the lacklustre appeal of
yesterday's action series had to do with its one-track plot.
The crime-fighter is single minded in his pursuit of the
criminal. He's got no personal life to sidetrack him. He's
got no agenda other than the case at hand. The newer
series are multi-faceted and more interesting to watch. In
La Femme Nikita, there's the love interest between Nikita
and Section One's top operative, Michael. In *Alias* you've
got spy action, family drama and romance. In *NYPD Blue*
you've got the personal problems of its protagonists.
These different elements spice up the show.

Though Michael Knight and KITT made a handsome
combination back in the 1980s, they just don't cut it
anymore in this day and age. Like big hairdo and shoulder

pads, they're best tossed out. For now, it's *Alias* on the menu. The future may tell a different story though. If you ask me to have a Pepsi Blue then, I may say, "That's so old-fashioned and uncool. Give me a Pepsi Rainbow!" Just moving with the times.

a bollywood recipe

I HAVE SAT through dozens of Bollywood movies and have come up with this perfect concoction for a hit.

Ingredients
- A beautiful Bollywood actress
- A handsome Bollywood actor
- A melodramatic mother
- A moustachioed father
- A comical sidekick
- A cunning uncle
- A police inspector with a baton
- 10 burly bad guys
- 18 back-up dancers
- Four 10-minute song-and-dance routines
- Plenty of romance
- A wet scene
- Some fighting
- 24 changes of costumes

Directions
1. Take a gorgeous Bollywood actress with long straight hair like Aishwarya Rai or Rani Mukherjee and let her meet a handsome Bollywood actor, preferably one

with muscles like Salman Khan or one with a cute face like Shah Rukh Khan.

2.   Let them sing and dance to their hearts' content, preferably for at least 10 minutes per song. Sprinkle these songs liberally throughout the movie. These should take place in the earlier part of the movie when the protagonists fall in love with each other. (The latter part of the movie would concentrate on the conflict and its resolution.) Bear in mind that the world has become a little global village. Don't confine them to cavorting around trees in the park. Go international. Let the protagonists teleport themselves to anywhere they want to be at a bob of the head and a shake of the bum. From the rolling fields of Mumbai to the snowcapped mountains of Switzerland, from the busy streets of Calcutta to the beautiful lakesides of Canada, anything is possible.

3.   Costume changes are essential for every new locale they appear in. Modern and traditional attire can be interchanged with each other.

4.   Don't forget to add the group of back-up dancers. They may pop up at the snap of the fingers. Just make sure they are clad in identical outfits and are physically fit to perform their gruelling dance routines. Refer to Michael Jackson's *Beat It* video for an idea of dance choreography. Precise coordination is a vital ingredient here. Nobody must move a finger out of sync.

5.   If you are feeling a little tired, you may take a short break. Go check your e-mail, take a shower or water the plants. By the time you return, the song would be ending and you can resume with the rest of the recipe.

6.   For a successful movie, songs must be of good quality. Whether they are fast-paced, catchy numbers or sentimental songs, they must have an echoing resonance to it. It does not matter if the song is to be sung on a helicopter or a boat where there's no possibility of any echoes bouncing off.

7.   While the song-and-dance is going on, mix in some tantalising scenes of the hero and heroine getting really close to each other as if they're going to kiss. Right at the last second, let them pull away. Remember, it is taboo for lips to meet in a Hindi movie.

8.   Build in a wet scene. This is where the heroine will get wet, either from being caught in the rain or having fallen into a river or fountain.

9. For some melodrama, have a pleasantly plump mother wringing her hands in despair while tears roll down her cheeks. Juxtapose her with a stern, moustachioed father, and it would complete the picture of a perfectly normal family.

10.   Stir in liberal doses of humour in the form of a comical sidekick who has perfected the art of exaggerated gestures. He or she can be the friend or servant of the protagonist.

11.   Throw in some bad guys. It could take the form of an evil uncle out to wrest the inheritance from the hero or a rival love interest out to wreak havoc. These characters must possess the ability to make their lips curl and eyes squint in a sinister manner. Also compulsory is their band of burly cohorts; ten would be a respectable number.

12.   For the fighting scenes, blows and punches are usually loud enough to be heard in the next block. It is

acceptable for the sounds of "kapish" and "kapow" to be heard before the punches land on the opponent. Exaggeration is also normal, so don't be alarmed if a slap on the face sounds like a karate-chop on a block of wood.

13.   Let the baton-wielding police inspector arrive in his jeep at a crucial moment. He could be just on time to watch the final showdown but for some strange reason, he would choose not to interfere until they have slugged it out. It's better if he arrives after the action is over. The bad guys would be sprawled all over the ground and he'd just have to handcuff the number one villain—that is, if he's not dead yet.

14.   Love always triumphs in the end. The hero wins the hand of his beloved. Let hero and heroine run to each other in slow-mo, with her scarf or sari flying in the wind. They fall into each other's embrace and the hero would spin her round and round. Ahh ... so romantic.

15.   Now sit back and enjoy.

CHORES,
CHORES,
CHORES

time to junk 'em

MY MUM is a hoarder. My grandma is a thrower. I'm somewhere in between.

Mum's house is stashed with stuff in every corner. The top of the kitchen window ledge houses an array of boxed pots and pans wrapped up neatly in plastic bags. The kitchen cabinet is bursting with crockery, cutlery, beverage tins and plastic containers. Her cupboards are so well-utilised that the tops are stacked with packages right up to the ceiling. Her sewing corner resembles a junkyard with a mountain of baskets, boxes and bags of toys, textiles and clothes threatening to collapse at the slightest disturbance.

In comparison, grandma's house is very spartan and spick and span. She doesn't need extra cabinets or drawers to store things. Everything is there for a purpose. Anything superfluous is thrown away. There aren't any boxes or bulging plastic bags hiding in this corner or that.

I have a bit of my mum and grandma in me, depending on the season. For 11 months of the year, my mum's hoarding habit resides in me, though to a lesser extent. (She even saves styrofoam lunch boxes!) I have this phobia of discarding things which I think might come in handy in the near future. Let's see, there's the collection of boxes—the mooncake box, shoe boxes, the box the thermos pot came in, the sturdy blue pewter box, the light bulb box. You never know when you need to gift wrap a present and having a suitable box available is like finding a fifty-ringgit bill when you are penniless.

There are loads of other stuff too. The kids' old socks waiting for me to turn into cute little puppets, old magazines stacked up in the cupboard lest I should need them as reference material for some writing project, empty jam jars that I could use to distribute homemade cookies to family and friends, and the stainless steel spine of a broken office chair which might come in useful if another such chair should fall apart.

I can't possibly list them all down, otherwise this will read like a scrap-yard inventory. Invariably these things are never used and only hog valuable space—until a month before Chinese New Year when the spring-cleaning bug is in the air. That's when my grandma's practice would reign supreme and I would go into a frenzy of cleaning and chucking.

First place to tackle is the kitchen cabinets. Empty margarine tubs, plastic containers for chilli and kaya, lids of ice-cream boxes minus their tubs which have been used as dog dishes and mineral water bottles have never looked so unappealing. Where before they appeared utilitarian, now they seem absolutely rubbishy. Into the dustbin they go together with the jam jars.

The fridge is next. It's easy to put things into cold storage and then forget about it. There's a block of left-over red bean paste for making *tau sar* dumplings languishing in a corner. The bottle of mustard and BBQ sauce on the fridge door have been untouched for months. The Thousand Island dressing is swimming in a layer of water. Packets of seasoning from instant noodle packs and McDonald's tomato ketchup sachets invade the egg-tray.

This calls for operation "peer-and-dump". Peer at the expiry date and dump it if it has expired. This exercise frees up a quarter of my fridge space and that excludes the middle compartment which functions as a medicine cabinet.

Like my mum, I'm wont to keeping unfinished prescription for self-medication. Paracetamol, running nose syrup, cough mixture, flu tablets, over-the-counter medicine for stomach ailments and aspirin are neatly categorised into different trays for ease of use. As time progresses, the addition of new bags of medicine chucked in randomly threw order into chaos. Transparent plastic bags from the GP's clinics and opaque white ones from the paediatrician's turned the compartment into a mountainous white landscape of plastic bags and medicine bottles. Order is restored by throwing away two-thirds of the medicine which have outlived their shelf lives.

The utility room which doubles up as a sewing and laundry room is in danger of becoming a trash pile. It's so convenient to dump things there, out-of-sight and out-of-mind until spring-cleaning time when accumulated junk suddenly acquires a dirty aura.

Then I begin to notice things such as the long box that used to house my son's model ship collecting dust in a corner. I had saved it to store wrapping paper but the king of procrastination had prevented it from being taken upstairs where the wrappers stood exposed—you guessed it—in yet another box.

I spy the cardboard core of a depleted roll of PVC slumped behind the sewing machine. I had planned to make a spear for illustrating the Israelites' fight against Goliath for my Sunday School class, but the core is useless now. It's bent in the middle and won't stand a fighting chance against a midget, let alone a giant. The Black & Decker hand vacuum which last saw action three years ago stood forlorn in a small box, sporting an inch-thick layer of dust while waiting to be repaired.

It's time to pack up the junk and clear the cobwebs. Spring is coming.

ironing out the wrinkles

IT WAS A FORTNIGHT before my wedding day. My bridal gown had been chosen and a new pair of trousers tailored for my future husband to wear with his rented cream-coloured jacket. After collecting the trousers from the tailor, I decided to iron it so that it will look neat and crisp.

I laid the trousers gingerly on the ironing board. With a sense of anticipation, I pressed the iron onto the pants. Instead of producing a smooth sheen, the iron shrivelled up the trouser leg to make it look like pickled mango skin. Though that wasn't a bad omen foretelling a rocky marriage (not that I believe in such things), it did signal the beginning of my hate affair with that ubiquitous household utensil.

Ironing is a chore. My motto is "iron when in need." When hubby yells for his shirts or the children clamour for their school uniform or the laundry basket overflows with clean, crumpled clothes—whichever comes first, that's the time to bring out the ironing board.

Putting off the detested chore to the last minute has its repercussions. Some school days would see me frantically ironing the children's uniforms while they are in the shower. Then I have to cool down the uniforms before they can wear them. A fast solution is to place the

273

uniforms in front of a box fan set on maximum. A quicker fix is to cool it in front of an open fridge.

Usually I am not meticulous when it comes to ironing. The faster I get the job done, the better. One unusual day, the fastidious flu must have bugged me. I decided to iron the pocket lining of hubby's trousers. For my diligence, I was rewarded with a gaping hole. Serves him right for saying that I burn a hole in his pocket when there's no truth in it. I've proven him right for once, literally.

Ironing is a science. You have to apply the right temperature to the right fabric. Otherwise, you might end up with "pickled mango skin" or a hole if the heat is too high or wrinkles if the temperature is too low. To obtain best results, garments must be slightly damp. For dry iron users like me, this means sprinkling the clothes with a spray. This is extra work, so I don't do it. I can live with the less than perfect results because I'm not a perfectionist and neither is my family. If they are, they're most welcomed to do the job themselves.

I've dropped my iron a few times but it's still usable. The ironing board which had a suspended wall cabinet fall on it once, is still strong though it's now sloping about 20 degrees. If I start coveting for the latest cordless gizmo, I just have to think of grandma's ancient heavy wrought iron filled with smouldering coals to get the perspective right.

In her heyday, grandma was an ironing expert. The garments that went under the iron emerged satiny smooth. Needless to say, she didn't cut corners like me. Always looking for ways to "work smart", I've come up with some simple tips for saving time and work.

1.   Hang up clothes immediately after bringing them in from the clothes line instead of letting them gather more wrinkles in the laundry basket.

2.   When ironing school blouses, press the collar, sleeves and shoulders only. Don't bother with the other parts as they stay out of sight under the pinafore.

3.   Same principle goes for shirts. Ignore shirttails as they're tucked into trousers.

4.   Refrain from pressing trousers too hard on high heat or they will acquire an unsightly sheen after a while. It will also show up the seams.

5.   Send difficult-to-iron clothes to the *dhobi* for professional services.

Keep pressing on, my friends.

farm them out

HAVING four children is considered one too many by today's standards. In our forefathers' time, it was too few. Most of them had "football-team" families. Yet they coped and see how well our parents turned out.

So how do I cope with four kids, a husband, two dogs and no maid? Easy. Farm them out. No, not the kids or husband or dogs, but the tasks that can be delegated to others.

The *numero uno* job that has to go is heavy-duty housework. I employ a cleaning lady to sweep and mop the floor, wash the toilets, do the windows and clean the fans. That goes a long way towards ensuring my sanity so I needn't dash around like a lunatic. When my cleaning lady had to go back to Indonesia for two months, at a perfectly wrong time immediately after the birth of my fourth baby, chaos reigned supreme.

On top of having a newborn to care for, I had to do the major housework plus all the other odds and ends that come with running a household. My children helped out whenever they could but their copious homework was a limiting factor. During those two months I shed the extra pounds gained from the pregnancy.

Mornings are always busy. Preparing my son for kindergarten, bathing the baby, washing the nappies and putting out the laundry take time. Since only my preschooler and I have lunch at home (my older kids have to stay back in school for tuition) I don't cook lunch. It's easier to *tapau* food from the coffeeshops. I figured out a way to buy food without having to bring the baby in and out of the car. I would drive up to my regular coffeeshop, wind down the window, shout out my order to the chicken-rice seller, then wait for my order to be delivered.

There is no love lost between the iron and I, especially when it comes to pressing my husband's office clothes. Somehow the shirts always end up with creases on one shoulder or the other. The best option is to send his clothes to the *dhobi* for ironing. It would be unprofessional for him to go to work in crumpled shirtsleeves. I don't want to be responsible for him getting a lousy increment from his boss for his unkempt dressing, so it's better to let some small bucks out so that the big bucks can come in.

Making several trips out of the house while lugging baby along is a hassle. I had to make four trips on most days. It would have been five if hubby did not send the older kids to school in the morning. The first trip takes my preschooler to the kindergarten. The second is for his return. The third trip is to fetch one child from primary school at one o'clock. The last trip at three-thirty is to fetch another who had to stay back for tuition in school.

My daughter has tuition from Wednesdays to Fridays. Eldest son's tuition are from Mondays to Thursdays. Hence the days when they both have tuition are Wednesdays and Thursdays, when I can pick them both at the same time. On other days, I would have to make separate trips at one and three-thirty.

As our house is quite a distance away from school—16 kilometres to be exact—it is difficult to find a car-pool for the kids. It is easier to arrange for transport to my mother's house, which is only about a kilometre from school. Whoever has no tuition will be sent to my mother's, thus eliminating the one o'clock trip. I round up both the children at half past three, one from the school, the other from my mum's.

It also helps that I'm pretty good at turning the proverbial blind eye. I pretend not to see the dust on my shelves until I have company coming to the house. Or the unfolded laundry in the baskets until the children run out of underwear. Or the coat of dust on my car until it's time to visit my in-laws. Or the clutter on the piano until hubby grumbles. Or the cockroach droppings in my kitchen sink cabinet until I simply cannot stand the sight and smell of them anymore.

If my eyes were to be wide open to all the housework to be done, life would be one endless list of chores from dawn to dusk. No, thank you. Life has more to offer than keeping the house spick and span all the time. Having said that, my house is not that messy. It has some semblance of order, if you close one eye.

LET'S TALK ABOUT THE WEATHER

the kai-tuck curse

I HATE Kai-Tuck the typhoon. According to the weather people, it's sucking up moisture from the air, making the weather drier. As if the current hot spell due to the southwest monsoon is not enough, this Kai-Tuck palaver is now giving us a double whammy of a sizzling weather.

In the afternoon, the thermometer reads 35°C on the upper floor of my house. It's as hot as a kitchen restaurant that has six stoves burning on the highest flame. If I were to stay downstairs on most afternoons, I wouldn't be bothered if it were as hot as the desert up there.

The problem is, I usually spend the afternoon upstairs because I have to use the computer for writing and surfing the Internet. As the computer is located upstairs, right next to the windows, I can feel the sun's hot tentacles reaching in through the lacy curtains and branding my skin with their heat.

After a few sweaty afternoons, I suggested to my better half to air-condition the living room upstairs. No way, he said. The area is too big and open; the air-con will not work efficiently.

How about getting an air-cooler then, I asked. No, he said, it's just not practical. At times like this, that chap deserves to be labelled my worse half.

This called for desperate measures to make living conditions more bearable in my scorching upper floor.

The first thing I did was to change the lacy curtains to opaque ones. When the afternoon sun hovers threateningly outside the windows, I put down the curtains. That helped cool down the place somewhat, from the equivalent of six burning stoves to five-and-a-half.

Not good enough, so I moved my computer far away from the windows to the other end of the room. If you have shifted a computer before, you'll know what a hassle the cables pose. They crisscross each other; from monitor to CPU, from CPU to UPS, from mouse to CPU, from keyboard to CPU, from CPU to speakers, from joystick .... The list is endless.

I did not relish having to sort out the cable puzzle later, so I figured it was best to move all the stuff as they were, with wires still attached.

All the hands available in the house were summoned. The cleaning lady carried the CPU, my daughter carried the speakers, my three-year-old son carried the joystick and I carted the monitor with the keyboard on top.

Gingerly, as if we were carrying a patient hooked up on a life-support machine, we inched three metres to the new destination. Surely, you can see now why I'm raving mad at Kai-Tuck, and an unrelenting husband who has a high tolerance of sizzling weather.

That is not all. There's the extra housekeeping to be done around the house. For starters, I have to make sure there's enough drinking water so the family doesn't end up dehydrated.

I'm relatively primitive and don't have those water filter gizmos that do away with boiling water, so water has to be boiled in a kettle over the gas stove. With the filled-up kettle weighing something like a 14in television set and having to lug the fat kettle around a few times a day is turning me into a possible contender for the next Mr. Universe competition.

Then there's the laundering work. You should see my children's clothes, especially those of my daughter who goes to afternoon school. She comes back with her white collar streaked with a black line as if she had used her Chinese paint brush to ink a line across. Pre-laundry spray, Fab and vigorous scrubbing are needed to remove the stain.

Outside my house, the trees planted by the town council are shedding more leaves than usual. Whilst I savour the shade they provide, the falling leaves mean more work. My driveway is strewn with hundreds of golden almond-shaped leaves that race each other every time a gust of wind blows.

These days, I've taken to wearing a hat, the type worn by Wilson, Tim Allen's next-door neighbour in the *Home Improvement* television sitcom. With a freckle-prone face, I gotta protect my not-so-perfect complexion from being speckled by the likes of Kai-Tuck. So I trot around town with a hat and sunglasses.

Malaysians who wear hats are usually found at high-society garden functions, out on the farm or the construction site. It's no wonder that I draw many stares since I don't belong to any of the above.

I've just read a newspaper report that says open burning is totally banned as the hot weather is expected to persist. I can't haul up Kai-Tuck by the collar—it's a typhoon for Pete's sake—but I can haul up a lighter-happy open-burner to the Department of Environment. I hope they slap him with a five-year jail sentence and a half-million ringgit fine. So, watch out when you see a woman in a cloth hat and sunglasses!

when it rains

I HAVE BEATEN the rain in a race.
Starting point: my son's school. Finishing line: my house.
Waiting in the car for my son to knock off from school,
big rain drops started to pelt down on the windscreen.
Uh-oh, my laundry was still out in the open.

I glanced impatiently at the clock in the car. It seemed
like an eternity before 12:59 turned to 1:00. *Kriinggg!* The
school bell went off. Students spilled out of the building
like ants on a march.

I revved up the engine while my son got into the car.
The minute he shut the door, I bolted off. I weaved in and
out of traffic like a Grand Prix driver.

Meanwhile the rain had gathered velocity. The wind
huffed and puffed. I had to turn the windscreen wipers to
maximum speed.

At the back seat, my son was clinging on to his seat.
On approaching a traffic light he said, "Mum, the light is
going to turn red!" I wanted to tell him "Son, yellow light
doesn't mean slow down. It means step on it," but I didn't. I
just grunted and made a sharp 90-degree turn just as the
lights turned red.

The closer I got to home, the lighter the rain became.
The wipers were switched to slowest speed. Eventually,
not a single drop of rain fell though the sky was overcast.

"Yipee! We made it!" I shouted as we arrived home. Junior rolled his eyes heavenwards.

Not only did I beat the rain but I also created a new record that day. The usual 15-minute journey from school to home clocked 12 minutes. This race has taken place a few times and I usually emerge the champion with dry laundry as the trophy.

Sometimes the rain and I play hide-and-seek. When rain comes seeking dry ground, I hide my laundry indoors. When the rain hides in clouds, I put the laundry out. On a cloudy day when the rain is as fickle as a woman shopping for clothes, I could end up making half a dozen trips in and out of the backyard.

When the rain evolves into a thunderstorm, it is a different ballgame altogether. Once I saw an electricity cable snapped by a falling tree branch in a thunderstorm. The cable leaped and danced as if it had a life of its own. Exploding sparks from the severed cable illuminated the night sky like fireworks. It was beautiful but eerie. The nearby row of shops experienced power surges causing the lights to blink on and off like Christmas trees. Fortunately, nobody was hurt in the incident.

On another occasion, I was watching television when a crack of thunder clapped, and zap! I saw a flash running from the electricity cables outside into my living room.

The television blacked out but it survived the onslaught. The microwave oven was not so lucky though. The electronic keypad went haywire. The convection function had been zapped and I couldn't use the oven for baking.

My computer was not spared either. Thankfully only the modem was knocked out and it didn't cost a bomb to buy a new one. A friend of mine didn't get it so good. His brand-new ten-thousand-ringgit computer system was wrecked by lightning. The last I heard, he was shopping around for a second hand computer.

More recently my electric gate was hit by this natural phenomenon which insurers classify as an "act of God". After a ferocious thunderstorm, the gate just refused to open. I called in the technician. After two hours of testing, he announced the verdict.

"You have to change the whole set of motor. It went up in smoke as I was testing it just now."

"Uh-oh. How much would that cost?"

"One thousand eight for the imported model."

I could see ringgit bills flying off with wings like in Master Q comics.

"Let me do some more testing," he said when I complained about the price.

It was a good thing he did because only the circuit board or something was spoilt. And my damage was only four hundred ringgit. I didn't haggle for a discount as I was so relieved. Mmmm, I wonder if that was a ploy to make me pay up happily?

Nowadays at the first rumble of thunder, I make a quick trip around the house, to switch off and unplug the computer, microwave, television and electric gate. Better to err on the side of caution.

A STROLL DOWN MEMORY LANE

always with me

IT HAS BEEN 30 years since my
maternal grandfather passed away. Though he flitted
through my childhood years, the short span of time I lived
with him meant more than the three decades of casual
relationship I had with my paternal grandfather.

Ah Kong was a lorry driver and opium smoker. When
he disappeared into the room with his bamboo pipe, I
knew he would be transported into a private world of his
own. As he lay on the wooden floor and indulged in his
habit, his face assumed a glazed and faraway look.

I was too young then to know what opium was. To
me, opium-smoking was part and parcel of Ah Kong. Like
his crew-cut silver hair and broad shoulders. Like the lump
of flesh on his shoulder blade which protruded like a
tennis ball. Like the teeny-weeny hole in that lump which
I dug with a pin. I didn't suppose he felt any pain as he sat
very still while I poked and probed. Even if it did, he
would not have complained, just to pander to my whim.

It touched me that Ah Kong always put my interest
first. We only had one toilet in the house. Once I needed
to use the toilet while he was doing his business. He
rushed out almost immediately, hands clutching his
dark-blue drawers with string still undone.

When I needed someone to soothe away the hurt, it
was Ah Kong to whom I turn. I remember an incident

when I had fallen off my bicycle when negotiating a sandy corner. My knee was grazed and a little bloodied but I put up a brave front. I sat under the porch and waited for Ah Kong to come home from work.

"What's this?" he asked as he bent down to inspect my knee when he returned. That was the cue for hitherto held-back tears to gush forth like a waterfall. No balm was more soothing than Ah Kong's concern.

To say Ah Kong was strong as an ox was no exaggeration. Effortlessly, he piggybacked 10-year-old me round the house and carried me to the bedroom when I had dozed off in the living room.

Back at a time when it was uncommon for men to bond with their offspring or grandchildren, Ah Kong and I were cementing our ties over the kitchen stove. On many a cold night, as he warmed his hands over an old tin of brewing leaves, he recounted stories from his childhood days.

Ah Kong was adopted by his parents when his adoptive mother had difficulty conceiving. Life was happy until biological children arrived on the scene and he became an outsider in the family.

Once he was asked to cut sheets of rubber with the promise of new clothes for the coming Chinese New Year. He didn't get them. His siblings did. Worse, he had to work through the festival. Ah Kong became rebellious. His father turned him out of the house at 16 when he refused to go to school. He took solace in opium.

To this day I'm not sure if his opium habit had led to his untimely demise. Mum said he had a gastritis attack at his workplace but nobody sent him to the hospital. He died curled up like a dried prawn.

The memory of that day remains fresh in my mind. I was waiting outside the house when the lorry carrying Ah Kong trundled up the village road. There in that lorry was my grandfather, my playmate, my comforter. And he was no more. I clutched the fence and cried.

I've heard older folks say that the spirit of the deceased always returns on the seventh day. After his funeral I laid an extra mattress beside me so that if his spirit should come home, he could come to rest beside me. I didn't feel his presence beside me that night. Or the next. I didn't realise it then but he was *with* me and will always be.

the rough-and-tumble years

I WAS a stilt-walker at ten. The stilts were rudimentary contraptions put together by my fifth uncle: two long poles with a wooden wedge nailed about two feet from the bottom of each pole.

Learning to walk on stilts was somewhat like learning to ride a bicycle. I climbed up on the stilts, holding tightly to the top of the poles. I took a few quick steps, and hastily dismounted when I started to wobble. After many practice sessions, I was good enough to race with fifth uncle and the neighbourhood children.

Even though fifth uncle was only fifteen at that time, he was very adept at carpentry. He built a little shed outside the wooden house where I lived with my grandparents. The shed was more like a bench for two with the roof and walls fashioned out of thick transparent plastic sheets draped over four poles. We sat outside in the evenings and observed the goings-on in the village. On rainy days it was especially fun to be cocooned inside the shed while watching the rain run down the plastic sheets.

Our village was located near the river, so it wasn't surprising that fifth uncle decided to build a boat. Using rough pieces of plywood, he constructed a little squarish sampan. When it was completed, we dragged it to the riverbank. We made our way through the mound of rubbish dumped at the slope and slowly pushed the boat into the river. Before we could even lift a leg to get in, it sank into the muddy Klang River. Obviously fifth uncle was unschooled in the mechanics of boatbuilding.

It wasn't all rough and tumble. I played house with my youngest aunty, four years my junior, and the two young girls who lived opposite our house. We used plastic toy crockery to play *masak-masak* (cooking) in their shady compound, using dried brown leaves as vegetables. Sometimes I caught a glimpse of the girls' mother in the dark interior of their house, pottering about in nothing more than her underwear.

In the 1970s, not every household could afford a television set. Ah Yong's family, who lived at the end of our row, was one of the privileged few who owned one. At night, aunty and I would make a beeline for their house to watch programmes such as *Get Smart* and *I Love Jeannie*. They always switched off the lights in the living room when the television set was on, creating a cinematic atmosphere. The highlight of our television-viewing was eating cakes freshly baked by Ah Yong's elder sister.

Even though my grandparents couldn't afford a television set, they did own a record player. I spent much time listening to the records of my fifth uncle and third aunty. Fifth uncle had six years of English education before he called it quits, so naturally he liked to listen to English songs. One of his favourite singers was Johnny Horton whose songs grew on me. Till today I can still remember the lyrics to "All for the love of a girl" and "North to Alaska".

Third aunty was Chinese-educated, so she only bought Chinese records. A popular singer during that era was Yau Soo Yoong, a petite woman with short, straight hair and powerful vocals. She was famous for the hit song "*Jin Tian Bu Hui Jia*" ("Not Coming Home Today"). Thanks to Yau Soo Yoong, my Mandarin was better than my classmates whose only brush with the language was during Pupil's Own Language (POL) classes.

The occasional mischief that I got into made my childhood all the more memorable.

At one time, third aunty's brother-in-law came to stay with us for some time. I disliked him because he liked to tease me. He was a young man with shoulder-length hair, muscular shoulders and tattoos on his arms. Strong as he appeared to be, every morning would see him curled up tightly in his blanket. I thought of a unique way to avenge myself of his teasing. One morning while he was cocooned in his blanket, I crept into his room with my weapon, a nail clipper. Fortunately his feet stuck out from beneath the blanket. I yanked out the hairs from his toes. He awoke with a start and chased me around the house.

At another time, grandmother rented out a room to a middle-aged childless couple. Most of the time they kept to themselves. I was curious to know what went on behind the locked door. When I could no longer bear the suspense, I peeped in through the crack of the room's wooden windows. The couple had just returned from work and were changing their clothes. Tickled by the sight, I fled the scene lest my giggles exposed me.

Over twenty years have passed since I moved out of the village. Unlike the murky waters which flowed through the Klang River, my childhood memories are as clear as the rain which streamed down the plastic sheets of fifth uncle's little shed.

contentious siblings

THIS YEAR, all three of my schoolgoing children are in afternoon school. Logistically, this is good because it reduces the number of trips to school. Environmentally, this is bad as two teenagers, one seven-year-old and a toddler produce enough noise pollution to rival that of a boisterous class of 40.

Sometimes, play becomes too rowdy and squeals of laughter turned into loud wails. Sometimes, it's a shouting match or feet stamping or "Mummy! He beat me!" or "Mummy! She said I'm stupid!"

I feign deafness. Otherwise, my head would start to pound and my heart constrict. I wish I could lock them all up in a soundproof room and let them tear each other to pieces. If you're not a mother, you think that's cruel. Mothers would agree with me. They may even harbour more sadistic thoughts.

But really, I should be thankful that my children weren't as contentious as my five siblings and I were in our younger days. Our parents used to punish us with the cane and belt (for the boys only) and made us kneel on the floor for ages.

Like other children in our era, we were "do-re-mi" kids, one born after the other in quick succession. Family planning, whether in quantity or spacing-out were almost

unheard of in those days. It wasn't uncommon for people
to have 12 children in as many years. As for us, it was six in
a span of eight years.

We had our share of altercation, quarrels and fights.
Many differences were threshed out physically. The girls
pulled hair, pinched and clawed. The boys resorted to
using the head and the mouth, the head as a battering ram
and the mouth for hissing out bad breath. The latter was
the *numero uno* weapon of a brother who shall remain
anonymous, and was extremely effective in making us turn
tail and run. Second brother was timid and thin but when
he was angry, the veins on his neck popped up like Bruce
Lee spoiling for a fight.

First brother knew how to hit where it hurts most.
One fight is etched in my mind, clear as a Polaroid shot.
We were standing in front of my cupboard where I kept
my treasured Enid Blyton books. He grabbed one and
ripped the pages across the middle. I yelled and lunged for
the book. He wouldn't let go. With his free hand, he
seized my T-shirt and pulled it till the front stretched out
like a tent. I taunted him to pull harder as it was his T-shirt
I was wearing. I can't remember how we resolved the
stalemate but the humour of the situation might have
dissipated it.

Humour. Now that's a quality that tends to shroud
many a memory lane. Second sister had a unique method
of keeping the younger ones in check. Though I'm the
eldest, she had that unenviable responsibility at that time
because first brother and I were in morning school,
leaving her to man the rest of the brood. To get them to
toe the line, she pretended to be mad. She crawled under

the bed with her armament of mosquito coil and sheets of paper.

"I'm going to eat mosquito coil and paper! Ha! Ha! Ha! Ha!" she announced and laughed maniacally from under the bed.

To show that she meant business, she shoved out "chomped" pieces of green coil and shreds of paper. To three young children, she sure sounded mad. She wasn't. She was just being creative. She has four sons today but she doesn't use such crazy disciplining methods anymore. If anything, she's into child development, going for child-raising seminars here and there.

Despite our differences and rivalry, we've had our fun. Second sister was the vivacious one amongst us. To entertain us, she would wear the yellow-and-white checkered skirt I sewed in home science class and perform an Indian dance complete with rolling eyes, bobbing head and swivelling limbs. We always ended up on the floor in stitches.

I was the quiet one with a book in hand. While I was immersed in the adventures of The Famous Five and The Secret Seven, my siblings were knee-deep in adventures, minus the crooks. They caught guppies in the drain near our house, dissected them and cooked them in an old milk tin over a small fire. They seized snails, smashed the shells and salted the creatures till they withered up and died.

Yep, those were the days, tinged with sepia that had softened the edges and diminished the noises. I look forward to the future when my cantankerous and contentious children will reminisce their childhood with nostalgia when their own offspring give them their come-uppance.

513

IT was 1969, the year I entered Standard
One. I remember the first few days of school. Surrounded
by a sea of strangers, scolded by a stern teacher and
overwhelmed by homesickness, I had never felt more
miserable in my life. Thankfully, my mother had
accompanied me to school during those early days. Just a
glimpse of her standing outside the classroom reassured
and calmed me, especially when my fierce teacher, Mrs.
Ng threatened to rap my knuckles if I could not count to
ten correctly.

As the days rolled into weeks, I began to get used to
the routine. Each morning when the bell rang, all the
students gathered at the school field to sing "Negara Ku".
During recess, I skipped rope with my newfound friends.
The days passed pleasantly enough except during
Arithmetics when Mrs. Ng scowled at me whenever I
fumbled with my counting. Or when people mistook me
for a Malay girl and spoke to me in Malay, an unfamiliar
language for me at that time.

One day my mother dropped me off at school as
usual before going off to work at the shoe factory. It was
just another day, or so I thought. Out of the blue, all sorts
of vehicles started to stream into the school compound.
Motorcycles, cars, bicycles, lorries even.

I nearly jumped out of my skin when the school bell suddenly rang. It had just rung a short while ago to signify the end of a period. My classmates and I looked at each other in bewilderment. Mrs. Ng, with an uncustomary worried look on her face, instructed us to carry on with our writing before she went out.

We were speculating on the reason for the sudden influx of people when a man stomped into our class. He was the father of one of my friends. He grabbed his daughter and dashed out of the class. Soon there were other parents outside the corridor and in the class. They scrambled to grab their own daughters and hurried off. There was no sign of Mrs. Ng. I was beginning to feel scared. What was happening? Was my mother coming to get me too?

"Ah Hong! Come out quickly!" a voice shouted.

I searched the crowd and saw a familiar face—my eldest uncle. I snatched up my rattan school bag and pushed my way out of the class. My uncle grasped my hand tightly.

"What's happening, Tua Ku? Where's mama?" I asked.

"People are fighting everywhere. Your mama's at home. She asked me to come and fetch you."

We squeezed our way down the staircase. With half the crowd climbing up and the other half descending, it was slow and arduous work. I was trailing behind my uncle as he led the way into the thronging sea of people. I felt his grip loosening on my sweaty palms. Someone shoved me from somewhere and I lost hold of my uncle's hand.

"Tua Ku! Tua Ku!" I shrieked, looking around frantically for him. I couldn't see him. All I saw were other

frenzied faces, some with girls in tow, others still
searching wildly for their own.

I was carried along by the jostling crowd like a ball
bobbing on a wave. I reached the parking lot and saw
people rushing off. A girl had fallen down and scraped her
knees on the gravelled ground. Another student dropped
her schoolbag into the drain, spilling out books from the
open rattan basket.

At the canteen, there was no sign of my uncle either. I
stood on a bench to get a better view. Suddenly I caught
sight of my uncle. Relief washed over me.

"*Aiya*! Why did you let go of my hand?" he chided
when I ran up to him.

I gave a teary smile and quietly clambered on to his
Vespa. I put my arms around his waist, afraid to fall off.
The motorcycle sputtered to life and threaded its way out
amidst the other vehicles and escaping people. The road
outside the school gate was packed. Fortunately, we could
weave our way out of the traffic jam easily on the Vespa.
We arrived home safe and sound.

That ugly day came to be known amongst the
Chinese as 513, for May 13, 1969, when racial riots
erupted in our nation and pandemonium reigned in my
school. I was too young to understand what was going on
then but the memory of that day makes me all the more
appreciative of the peaceful harmony we live in now.

confessions of a book addict

I WAS hit by a car while cycling to school one day. I was out of school for several days. When I returned to class, my thoughtful classmates presented me with two Enid Blyton books—*The Naughtiest Girl in the School* and *Second Form at Malory Towers*. To this day, I can still remember the cover of *The Naughtiest Girl in the School*. It showed a girl with a mop of curly brown hair with defiant sparkling eyes, standing with hands akimbo.

Despite what critics may say about Enid Blyton (her books have been criticised for their racism, sexism and snobbishness), she had done a great favour for young children the world over. Her stories of talking toys, gnomes, boarding school girls and young sleuths have captured the hearts of millions of children all over the world. I'm one of the beneficiaries who have acquired a love of reading thanks to her. I enjoyed all her books, though my favourites were the *Famous Five* and *Secret Seven* series.

Secondary school saw me moving on to young detective series like Caroline Keene's *Nancy Drew* and Franklin W. Dixon's *The Hardy Boys*. I spent so much time in the school library hunting down these books that the librarians saw it fit to rope me in as their secretary. When I got home from school, I had to have a book in hand before I could sit down comfortably for lunch.

The amateur sleuths later lost their appeal to Mr. Tall, Dark and Handsome of M&B books (initials stand for Maths and Biology when speaking in the presence of teachers; at other times they were known as Mills & Boon). I hogged the bookstands set up on five-foot ways. They rented out M&B books for 50 sen a pop which was still cheaper than paying three or four ringgit for a brand-new book.

At about this time, a Filipino family moved into our neighbourhood. The father was a bank manager and the pretty teenage daughter had an entire library of M&B and other romance novels. Gasp! I was like a toddler turned loose in a sweet shop. Gleefully I borrowed stacks of books at a time and devoured them till the wee hours of the morning. And my mother thought I was studying! Little did she know that I was ensconced in a saccharine romantic world spun by the likes of Janet Dailey, Denise Robins and Barbara Cartland.

After a while, the same old formula in the romance novels began to turn stale and predictable. I was up to my chin with the same old fluffy plots, the same old dashing heroes and swooning heroines, and cookie-cutter kissing scenes. I reached saturation point where one more helpless stammering heroine and one more aristocratic hero with inscrutable expression would make me scream like a banshee.

Exit Mr. Handsome and Ms. Pretty. Enter Arthur Conan Doyle's Sherlock Holmes and Agatha Christie's eccentric and fastidious Belgian detective Hercule Poirot and his "little grey cells". (I seem to have this thing for detective stories.) Their acute powers of observation and deduction earned my highest admiration. To this day, I'm wont to spout "Elementary, my dear Watson, elementary" when I wanted to sound clever. And not forgetting the kindly but shrewd and irrepressible Miss Jane Marple of St. Mary Mead, the English spinster who solves crimes without resorting to fancy high-tech gadgets, relying instead on her feminine sensitivity, empathy and intuitive intelligence.

Sixth form exposed me to the works of William Shakespeare, the Bront‰ sisters and poets like Alfred Tennyson and Robert Browning. I digested these works in the course of duty rather than the pleasure they could afford but I learnt to respect their skilful penmanship in critical appreciation class. These literature classes stood me in good stead later in life when I would voluntarily pick up copies of *Jane Eyre, Wuthering Heights* and *Emma* and read them with enjoyment.

When I joined the nine-to-five brigade, reading was relegated to the back burner. Still, I did find time for the occasional Sidney Sheldon, Arthur Hailey and Stephen King novels. When I became a mother, time became the scarcest of commodities. There was hardly time to catch my breath, let alone read a book. Reading had become a luxury.

I remember going on a special holiday once. Hubby had to attend a seminar in Singapore for a few days. I borrowed two thick novels from the library, left the children with my mum and tagged along with him to Singapore. While hubby was out, I holed myself in the hotel room and read till my vision blurred and my temples throbbed. When I went out to grab a bite, the book went with me. When I went down to the pool, I brought the book to read on the lounge chair. That was one unforgettable holiday. I hope some day soon, I'll have the opportunity to have another such break but it's going to take some working. Then I had only two kids, now there are four.

It is difficult to find time for reading books these days. If I do read them, they are confined to how-to books and short-story collections. Something like *The Elements of Copywriting* or *The World's Greatest Cranks and Crackpots*. These don't have the pull of page-turning novels like those of John Grisham's or Amy Tan's.

I can't resist a good yarn. I would become like an ostrich. Instead of the head being buried in the sand, mine would be stuck in the book. My eyes would be glued to the pages and my posterior to the chair. Meals would be served late. Children's whining ignored. Hubby's grumbling shut off. Television would have lost its lure.

Nothing can beat a good book.

LYDIA TEH was born and bred in Klang, Malaysia. She still resides in this royal town famous for its glittering streetlights, seafood, *bah-kut-teh* (herbal pork stew) and crows.

A former secretary, she enjoys writing while raising her brood of four. In between cooking for her children, chauffeuring them around and coaching them in their studies, she loves observing the quirks and idiosyncrasies of Malaysians. Though she dreams of tapping out a knockout novel from the comfort of a beach house or a cottage on a hill, she's just as happy writing at home, the library or the café.

Life's Like That: Scenes from Malaysian Life is her second book. Her first, *Congratulations! You Have Won!: A Guidebook on How to Maximize Your Chances of Winning Competitions*, was published in 2001.

Comments for Lydia Teh? You can reach her at *tehlydia@yahoo.com*

about the author